The American Revolutionary War in the south

A Re-evaluation from a British perspective in the light of The Cornwallis Papers

Ian Saberton

Grosvenor House
Publishing Limited

This book is published by
Grosvenor House Publishing Ltd
Link House
140 The Broadway, Tolworth, Surrey, KT6 7HT.

www.grosvenorhousepublishing.co.uk
info@grosvenorhousepublishing.co.uk

A CIP record for this book
is available from the British Library

ISBN 978-1-78623-154-3

About the author

Ian Saberton was educated at Firth Park Grammar School, Sheffield, and at the Universities of Birmingham and Warwick in the UK. He holds a PhD in history from the latter, having previously graduated with a BA (Hons) in Russian from the former. After translating technical Russian for the British Library, he entered the UK Government Service.

Perhaps of greatest relevance to his writing about the war in the south was his service as an adviser on constitutional and political affairs, machinery of government, contingency planning, devolution and the like in the Northern Ireland Office (NIO) at the height of the troubles. Part of his duties, as the highways and byways of the world were searched for lessons to be learnt, was to write historical papers of an applied nature for the benefit of Ministers. It is then that he became keenly interested in the American Revolution. Overall, what his service in NIO has brought to his re-evaluation of the southern campaigns is hands-on experience in dealing with a quasi-revolutionary situation. There are, despite the passage of years, distinct parallels to be drawn between the troubles and the revolutionary war in America.

The American Revolutionary War in the south

A Re-evaluation from a British perspective

in the light of The Cornwallis Papers

Contents

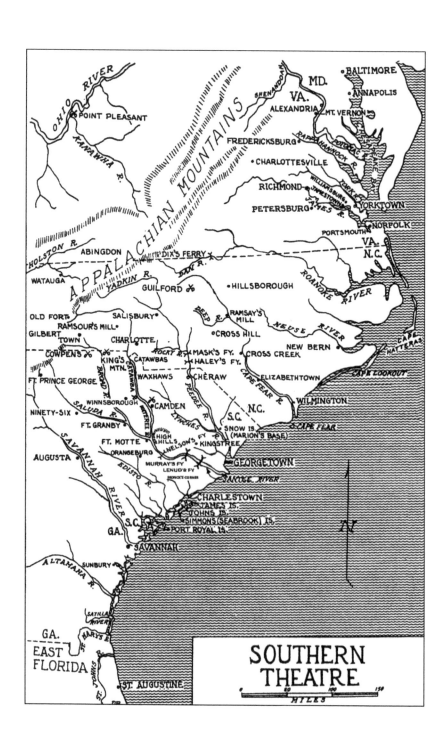

SOUTHERN
THEATRE

∞ 1 ∞

Was the American Revolutionary War in the south winnable by the British?

It was in 1975, when I was researching the American Revolution, that I came upon the Cornwallis Papers in the UK National Archives. I was much surprised that, despite the passage of almost 200 years and the vast extent of literature on the Revolution, no one had yet got around to editing and publishing this extraordinarily important primary material in so far as it related to the southern campaigns of 1780 and 1781 — material that in my estimation was crucial to evaluating the war in the south. I therefore decided to do the job myself.[1]

As published, *The Cornwallis Papers* has two purposes: first, to provide a comprehensive and fully edited transcript of the papers; and second, in view of the numberless inaccuracies littering the historical record, to provide a commentary, whether in the introductory chapters or various footnotes, aimed at presenting the papers in an accurate, balanced and dispassionate way. "Yet," as stated in the preface to volume I, "it is so very difficult to be accurate, balanced and dispassionate about a conflict in which political passions were so polarised and views so warped by them. Inevitably, it is the perspective from which the Papers are viewed which will to a degree determine whether the editor is seen to have squared the circle."[2]

---

[1] See Ian Saberton ed., *The Cornwallis Papers: The Campaigns of 1780 and 1781 in the Southern Theatre of the American Revolutionary War*, 6 vols (Uckfield: The Naval & Military Press Ltd, 2010) ("CP").

[2] CP, 1: ix.

Relying mostly on inferences drawn from my commentary in *The Cornwallis Papers*, I shall seek to demonstrate that Britain's grand strategy for reducing the southern colonies was at least in part sound and it may well have achieved a lasting measure of success if only Clinton, the British commander-in-chief, and Cornwallis, the GOC in the south, had played their cards right.[3] So what went wrong, beginning in June 1780, one month after the capture of Charlestown, as Clinton set sail from South Carolina for the north?

The cardinal sins were initially to underestimate to a gross extent the number of troops needed for prosecuting the campaigns, to misjudge the continued pacification of conquered territory, to omit taking into account the likely nature of the war should pacification not succeed, and to fail to improvise tactics accordingly — all contrary to Clausewitz's first rule of war: "The first, the supreme, the most far-reaching act of judgement that the statesman and commander have to make is to establish ... the kind of war on which they are embarking, neither mistaking it for, nor trying to turn it into, something that is alien to its nature. This is the first of all strategic questions and the most comprehensive."[4]

Of the number of troops left with Cornwallis — a number on which historians widely diverge — Mackesy provides a convincing account that 6,753 effectives remained in South Carolina and 1,706 in Georgia, of whom 4,870 and 1,259 were respectively fit for duty.[5] The upshot was that while posts at Camden, Cheraw Hill, the village of Ninety Six and Augusta were established, there were,

---

[3] For a summary of the strategy, see CP, 1: 3-4.
[4] Claus von Clausewitz, *On War*, edited by Beatrice Hauser (Oxford: Oxford University Press, 2008), 30.
[5] Piers Mackesy, *The War for America 1775-1783* (reprint of 1964 edition, Lincoln: University of Nebraska Press, 1993)., 346, quoting CO 5/100(53) (Kew: UK National Archives). In South Carolina Cornwallis took 2,500 men to Camden, and Balfour some 600 to Ninety Six, leaving three British and three Hessian regiments to garrison Charlestown. In Georgia were Allen's, Brown's, Cruger's and Wright's British American corps, together with von Porbeck's Hessian.

apart from the troops at Camden, precious few to control the vast hinterlands given the need to maintain the posts themselves. So the opportunity was there, which the revolutionaries seized, to regroup unopposed and to commence what became the insurgency. Far better to nip it in the bud, but where were the troops to do so?

As Gen. Samuel B Griffith has pertinently observed, though perhaps a little too negatively, "Historical experience suggests that there is very little hope of destroying a revolutionary guerrilla movement after it has survived the first phase [*organisation and consolidation*] and has acquired the sympathetic support of a significant segment of the population. The size of this 'significant segment' will vary; a decisive figure might range from 15 to 25 per cent."[6] As for controlling a population of some 83,000 in South Carolina's backcountry, the shortage of troops was in fact risible.[7] In the east some 700 men of the 71st (Highland) Regiment occupied Cheraw Hill, but were soon decimated by illness and disease. It was not long before they were withdrawn. In the west Lt. Col. John Harris Cruger soon superseded Lt. Col. Nisbet Balfour in command of the District of Ninety Six, but his and Lt. Col. Isaac Allen's corps amounted to no more than near 300 men fit for duty. In Georgia Augusta was shortly to be occupied by Lt. Col. Thomas Brown's corps alone, but it too amounted to no more than 200 men fit for duty, leaving the vast swathe of territory between there and Savannah totally bereft of troops.[8] Admittedly, part of the shortfall in Ninety Six was for a time countered by the formation of the royal militia, but grossly unsupported by regulars, it was inadequate to control large expanses of territory there.

---

[6] Introduction to Mao Tse-Tung, *On Guerrilla Warfare* (New York: Praeger Publishers Inc, 1961), 27.
[7] The figure of some 83,000 is taken from Carl Bridenbaugh, *Myths & Realities: Societies of the Colonial South* (reprint of 1952 edition, New York: Atheneum, 1976), 121.
[8] For biographical notes on Cruger, Balfour, Allen, and Brown, see CP, 1: 35-7, 258-9 and 271-2.

As far as other aspects of pacification are concerned, experience soon proved that in a politically polarised situation lenity was not the answer. Short of admitting failure, the only solution was to adopt a policy of deterrence, but none was in the main adopted by Cornwallis and in any event, to be effective, it would have had to depend on an adequate number of troops to back it up.

Of Cornwallis's lenity *The Cornwallis Papers* affords a number of examples. Captured at the Battle of Camden and in the action at Fishing Creek were a number of militiamen who had perfidiously sworn allegiance to the Crown, enrolled in the royal militia, and gone off to the enemy. Although all deserved the halter for their treachery, only "some few of the most hardened ... were actually executed." He did go on to order Cruger, Major Patrick Ferguson and Lt. Col. George Turnbull to execute persons of the same description, but mitigated his order by stating that, if there were many, only several of the ringleaders were to be hanged.[9] Needless to say, revolutionary propaganda malevolently exaggerated the extent of the executions and it has percolated down to the present day.

Another example was his treatment of those in the Long Cane settlement who, violating their paroles, went off to join Lt. Col. Elijah Clark and Col. Benjamin Few before participating in the action near White Hall. Defeated by Allen there, many begged to resume their paroles and were in fact pardoned by Cornwallis with no sanction whatever for their violations.[10]

When public order breaks down or is in danger of doing so, it has been the practice since time immemorial for the courts to impose deterrent sentences. If ever there was reason to adopt

---

[9] CP, 2: 19 and 20; Charles Stedman, *History of the Origin, Progress, and Termination of the American War* (London, 1792), 2: 214. For biographical notes on Ferguson and Turnbull, see CP, 1: 37-8 and 138-9.

[10] For biographical notes on Clark and Few, together with an account of the action near White Hall, see CP, 1: 257, and 3: 282-3. For Cornwallis's lenity, see CP, 3: 286-7.

such a policy, it was in the backcountry of South Carolina in 1780, for, if the full rigour of martial law were not imposed, leaving transgressors to escape with impunity, how was it possible to deter parolees, protectioners, and those who had submitted from taking up arms? Yet Cornwallis proceeded otherwise.

As to deterrence, it is unnecessary for me to expatiate except to assert a perhaps self-evident and simple fact, namely that a principal purpose is to deter by threat or way of punishment actions or omissions of a particularly injurious nature.

Then there was Cornwallis's treatment of the loyalists, who according to Col. Robert Gray, a most percipient commentator, constituted about fifty percent of the backcountry population. Over the past five years they had been brutally repressed by the revolutionary authorities and demanded retribution. By not providing it — except to exile certain deposed officers and officials to the sea islands for other reasons — Cornwallis alienated his friends without winning over his enemies.[11]

When we consider retributive justice, as sought by the loyalists, it embraces in its classical form the idea that the amount of punishment should be proportionate to the amount of harm caused by criminally offensive behaviour. Despite criticism in recent years the concept remains to this day a central pillar of the criminal law, and it is perhaps right that it should be so, for, if individuals begin to believe that society is unwilling or unable to impose penalties commensurate with injurious acts, then seeds of anarchy and vigilante justice are sown. Indeed, it was the lack of retributive justice that impelled many loyalists to seek vengeance on their enemies, thereby adding to the disorder in the backcountry.

---

[11] Robert Gray, "Col. Robert Gray's Observations on the War in Carolina", *The South Carolina Historical and Genealogical Magazine*, 11 (July, 1910), 139-59, 148, previously published in the *North Carolina University Magazine*, 8, No. 4 (November, 1858), 145-60. For a biographical note on Gray, see CP, 1: 135.

As respects the likely nature of the war should pacification not succeed, the British had a wealth of experience in meeting with aroused irregular opposition, for example at Concord and Lexington, and not least in the comprehensive defeat of Burgoyne. Wherever the British campaigned, it had become a fact of life. This being so, it was naive to assume that it would not break out in the south and to fail to plan ahead. In the plains and open woodlands there, the key to defeating irregulars was mounted troops, as Major George Hanger, who served in the south, explained: "The crackers and militia in those parts of America are all mounted on horseback, which renders it totally impossible to force them to an engagement with infantry *only*. When they chuse to fight, they dismount and fasten their horses to the fences and rails; but if not very confident in the superiority of their numbers, they remain on horseback, give their fire, and retreat, which renders it useless to attack them without cavalry, for though you repulse them and drive them from the field, you can never improve the advantage or do them any material detriment." Yet the only mounted troops Cornwallis was left with were the British Legion and a detachment of the 17th Light Dragoons. Their numbers were totally inadequate for such a job. As Robson succinctly put it, "The British, hidebound by their European background, never improvised sufficiently." Without improvisation and adaptation to American conditions they were in no position to succeed.[12]

And so, as 1780 progressed, a combination of the above factors led the British to control neither the entire eastern part of

---

[12] The Hon George Hanger, *An Address to the Army in reply to Strictures of Roderick M'Kenzie (late Lieutenant in the 71st Regiment) on Tarleton's History of the Campaigns of 1780 and 1781* (London, 1789), 82; CP, 2: 34; Eric Robson, *The American Revolution in its Political and Military Aspects 1763-1783* (reprint of 1955 edition, New York: W W Norton & Co Inc, 1966), 99. "Crackers" were a body of hardy, illiterate and lawless backwoodsmen scattered among the backcountry population. Feared more than most by the British, they tended to have no settled habitation and lived partly by hunting and partly by preying on their neighbours.

South Carolina by the close of the summer nor, with the defeat of Ferguson, almost the whole of the backcountry by the close of the year.

Finally, when reviewing what went wrong, we need to take into account Cornwallis's precipitate invasions of North Carolina without first consolidating control of South Carolina and Georgia in line with Clinton's instructions;[13] his continuance of the second invasion after the defeat at Cowpens; and his absurd and fateful decision at Wilmington to forsake the provinces to the south and march into Virginia.

As events would prove, the autumn campaign of 1780, in which North Carolina was penetrated for the first time, was a very risky venture indeed, yet despite the operational difficulties attending it, Cornwallis saw no option but to go on to the offensive. As he had explained to Clinton, "It may be doubted by some whether the invasion of North Carolina may be a prudent measure, but I am convinced it is a necessary one and that, if we do not attack that province, we must give up both South Carolina and Georgia and retire within the walls of Charlestown."[14]

Of the risks Cornwallis was running, the greatest was that of losing control of much of South Carolina and Georgia, so few were the troops that he left behind. Charlestown and Savannah were safe, but what about the rest of the country? If we leave aside the relative backwater of Georgetown, there were only three principal posts outside Charlestown and Savannah — at Camden, the village of Ninety Six, and Augusta. Left to garrison Camden were the New York Volunteers and the South Carolina Royalist Regiment under the overall command of Turnbull, who, in the words of Cornwallis, "tho' ... not a great genius, ... is a plain rightheaded man." If we subtract the troops intended to reinforce Cornwallis, those remaining at Camden amounted to no more than 250 fit for duty, far too few to maintain the post,

---

[13] See Clinton to Cornwallis, 1 June 1780, CP, 1: 56-9.
[14] Ibid., 177.

control the extensive hinterland, and, not least, provide support for the royal militia, without which, if attacked, it was an edifice waiting to crumble. At Ninety Six and Augusta those other most capable officers, Cruger and Brown, had equally few troops and faced the same parlous situation.[15]

It was at Charlotte that matters came to a head and the campaign was terminated due to unforeseen events. The first of these was the entirely unexpected ferocity with which the inhabitants of the locality continued resolutely to oppose the occupation of Charlotte itself.[16] On 3 October Cornwallis commented to Balfour, now the Commandant of Charlestown, "This County of Mecklenburg is the most rebellious and inveterate that I have met with in this country, not excepting any part of the Jerseys."[17] It soon became apparent that the village was completely unsuitable for a small intermediate post, so effectually would it have been blockaded and so high would have been the risk of its being taken out in detail. Preoccupied with defending itself, the post would have exerted no control over the surrounding territory and afforded no protection to messengers coming to and from Cornwallis as he pursued his onward march. Extraordinarily difficult as it already was to communicate with South Carolina (almost all of the messengers being waylaid), Cornwallis faced the prospect of totally losing the communication if he proceeded farther. He nevertheless contemplated advancing as late as the 11th, but as Col. Francis Lord Rawdon[18] explained to Balfour, the lack of communication with South Carolina brought about by the inveteracy of the Mecklenburg inhabitants, the uncertainty of cooperation with a diversionary force intended for the Chesapeake, and the possible consequences of a second event of calamitous proportions convinced

---

[15] CP, 2: 28-30.
[16] See, for example, Banastre Tarleton, *A History of the Campaigns of 1780 and 1781 in the Southern Provinces of North America* (London, 1787), 159-61, and Hanger, *An Address to the Army*, 66-70.
[17] CP, 2: 106.
[18] For a biographical note on Rawdon, see CP, 1: 151-2.

him that he had to turn back. He quit Charlotte at sunset on the 14th.[19]

The second event was the defeat of Ferguson. Why, as he became increasingly aware of the formidable force gathering to oppose him, he did not press ahead to join Cornwallis has long remained a puzzle. The answer may at first have lain partly in his having ideas beyond his station, that is to say, in his reluctance to forego a separate command, which he had previously exercised on more than one occasion, and partly, as evinced by *The Cornwallis Papers*, in his belief that he could take on and defeat his opponents himself. If initially the answer, it was eventually overtaken by another as Ferguson began to realise that his hopes of success were doubtful. Taking post on 6 October at King's Mountain, "where I do not think that I can be forced by a stronger enemy than that against us," he called for 2 or 300 of Col. Matthew Floyd's militia to join him the following evening unless they were destined for another service.[20] With such a reinforcement "we do not think ourselves inferior to the enemy if you are pleas'd to order us forward; but help so near at hand, it appear'd to me improper of myself to commit any thing to hasard." It soon became clear that he was egregiously mistaken in believing that the risks of advancing outweighed for the time being those of remaining where he was. The terrain at King's Mountain proved ideal for an onslaught by revolutionary irregulars and he was totally defeated in the afternoon of the 7th. Ferguson was killed and his entire party consisting of his corps — the American Volunteers — and some 800 militia was captured or killed.[21]

Cornwallis for his part was not free of blame for the disaster. The war had shown that detachments such as Ferguson's were ever attended with danger and had thrown up various instances of their fatal and ruinous effects. While, admittedly, having sound reasons for not reinforcing Ferguson offensively,

---

[19] CP, 2: 30, 106, 126 and 251.
[20] For a biographical note on Floyd, see CP, 1: 142.
[21] CP, 2:, 30-1 and 159-65.

Cornwallis appears to have taken no account — at least in the short term — of the need to support him for defence.

Nothing is so certain as the unexpected, and it was the unexpected, magnifying the risks of losing territory to the south, that ultimately put paid to the northward invasion.

It is easy to be wise after the event when we look back on the autumn campaign, but the question is not so much why the campaign was delayed — to which my commentary in *The Cornwallis Papers* provides the answers[22] — as why it ever took place. The plan was devised when South Carolina was in a quiescent state. As long as it remained so, it seemed reasonable to assume that public order could be maintained by leaving relatively few troops in support of the royal militia. Yet by the time that the campaign began the situation had markedly worsened. The territory east of the Wateree and Santee was in open revolt, the backcountry had been the scene of various actions and might be so again, and much of the royal militia was not to be relied on. In the light of the changed circumstances it was folly to throw caution to the winds and proceed with the original plan, for, self-evidently, much was to be lost if success or failure in North Carolina was vitiated or attended by losing control of even more territory than had already been lost to the south. Overall, as belatedly recognised by Cornwallis when he brought Major Gen. Alexander Leslie to join him,[23] it would have been far better if he had abandoned the campaign before it began and simply called for a reinforcement, but here again the prime concern should have been to use it for consolidating British authority in the two provinces so tenuously held rather than for pursuing wildcat ventures to the north.

Propelling Cornwallis to precipitate action was the political imperative of making progress swiftly. Unfortunately for him, he struck the wrong balance between political and military considerations, acted prematurely, and the collapse of the campaign almost inevitably ensued.

---

[22] Ibid., 25.
[23] For a biographical note on Leslie, see CP, 3: 3-4.

My preceding critique applies equally to the winter campaign, when North Carolina was invaded again. Strategically it was wrong to begin the campaign, and even worse to continue with it after Cowpens, for, by destroying his extensive train of baggage and provisions, Cornwallis was perforce unable, unless resupplied, to remain in the back parts of North Carolina, a prerequisite if the loyalists were to embody. It almost beggars belief that, with the North Carolinians in Lt. Col. John Hamilton's corps available to advise, his intelligence was so poor as not to indicate that the only means of resupply, by water from Wilmington to Cross Creek, was impractical.[24]

It is at Wilmington, when we analyse Cornwallis's decision to forsake the provinces to the south and march into Virginia, that we realise how unsuited he was to command in a conflict so akin to a civil war. Prior to the publication of *The Cornwallis Papers* his decision had puzzled historians for almost 230 years and none had come close to determining his real motives. Almost all, like Alden, Gruber, Lumkin, Mackesy, Peckham and Tonsetic, had simply accepted the decision at face value or as no more than a strategic mistake, while a few, like Pancake and Rankin, had attempted to justify it on spurious grounds such as assuring the safety of the Carolinas by disrupting Greene's supplies and reinforcements or as making the Chesapeake the main focus of the war.[25]

---

[24] For a biographical note on Hamilton, together with a description of his corps, see CP, 1: 55.

[25] John R Alden, *The American Revolution 1775-1783* (reprint of 1954 edition, New York: Harper & Row, 1962), 238; idem, *A History of the American Revolution* (London: Macdonald and Co, 1969), 465; Ira D Gruber, "Britain's Southern Strategy," in W Robert Higgins ed., *The Revolutionary War in the South: Power, Conflict, and Leadership* (Durham NC: Duke University Press, 1979), 205-38, 235; Henry Lumkin, *From Savannah to Yorktown: The American Revolution in the South* (St Paul, Minn: Paragon House, 1981), 223; Mackesy, *The War for America*, 407-8; Howard H Peckham, *The War for Independence: A Military History* (reprint of 1958 edition, Chicago: University of Chicago Press, 1973), 177; Robert L Tonsetic, *1781: The Decisive Year of the Revolutionary War* (Hovertown PA: Casemate, 2013), 105-6; John S Pancake, *This Destructive War: The British Campaign in the Carolinas, 1780-1782* (reprint of 1985 edition, Tuscaloosa:

In what Borick has described as among my "most ground-breaking and insightful analysis"[26] I have sought to disprove, by drawing on *The Cornwallis Papers* alone, Cornwallis's contention that it was impracticable for him to return overland to South Carolina. I have gone on to analyse his stated reasons for not moving that way and concluded that they do not hold water. This being so, I have advanced what in my estimation were most likely the real reasons propelling him to take the absurd and fateful decision that he did, besides explaining why the whole affair evinced "at best a serious flaw in his character and at worst a gross dereliction of duty." In short, Cornwallis was temperamentally ill at ease with defensive warfare, a prospect facing him if he returned to South Carolina and Georgia; a humane, cultivated man, he was sickened by the murderous barbarity with which the war was waged there by the revolutionary irregulars and state troops; he had no stomach for the deterrent and necessarily disagreeable measures involved in suppressing the rebellion there; and he was suffering from the mental and physical fatigue of commanding a year's hard and solid campaigning. Against this background it is not entirely surprising that he should have cast around, perhaps subconsciously, for reasons to release him from the predicament of dealing with a situation which he had come to detest. Always keen to act offensively, he simply opted for the more congenial alternative of doing so in Virginia, well way from the distasteful nature of the war farther south, an alternative, incidentally, which pricked his pride less than the perceived ignominy of conducting a defensive war to the southward after another unsuccessful campaign. These, then, were most likely the real reasons why Cornwallis took the absurd and fateful decision that he did.[27]

University of Alabama Press, 2003), 189-90; Hugh F Rankin, "Charles Lord Cornwallis: Study in Frustration," in George Athan Billias ed., *George Washington's Generals and Opponents: Their Exploits and Leadership* (Boston MA: Da Capo Press, 1994), part II, 213.

[26] Carl P Borick, Review, *The South Carolina Historical Magazine*, 112, Nos 1-2 (January-April 2011), 88-90, 89.

[27] For the a full analysis of Cornwallis's decision and his motivation, see CP, 4: 101-3.

However much we may sympathise with his reasons, more weighty considerations were involved. It is no exaggeration to say that his decision was critical in a series of events that lost Britain the southern colonies and cost it the entire war.

And yet, as I shall now demonstrate, the British might have achieved a lasting measure of success, notwithstanding the limited number of troops available in North America,

Admittedly, it was only natural for Clinton to be concerned about the arrival of the French expeditionary force and the threat to New York, but wars are won, not by cautious, hesitant commanders, but by those who are prepared to take risks. Instead of taking about 4,500 troops with him to New York, he should have left them with Cornwallis in keeping with the primacy of the southern strategy.[28] Well garrisoned with some 15,500 effectives, of whom some 10,000 were fit for duty, New York should have been able to hold out if attacked, and in any event till reinforced from the south.[29]

With such an accretion of force Cornwallis would — perhaps at once, as seems inevitable — have assigned it to the backcountry, maybe half to Ninety Six and half to the east of South Carolina, thereby providing badly needed support for the royal militia and deterring the revolutionary irregulars from regrouping. Of particular value would have been the Queen's Rangers,[30] who were among the troops recalled to New York, though the

---

[28] The figure of about 4,500 is provided by Clinton in his *The American Rebellion*, edited by William B Willcox (New Haven: Yale University Press, 1954), 191, footnote 6.
[29] What would have constituted the New York garrison if about 4,500 troops had not been brought from South Carolina is based on subtracting the latter figure from those for the garrison provided by Mackesy in his *The War for America*, 346.
[30] Like the British Legion the Queen's Rangers was a British American corps, part cavalry, part infantry. Commanded by Lt. Col. John Graves Simcoe, it was formed in 1777 and used for light and active service. It had taken part in the Charlestown campaign.

shortage of cavalry was so abysmal that a wise decision would have been to supplement them and the cavalry remaining in South Carolina — that is to say, the British Legion and a detachment of the 17th Light Dragoons — with mounted troops formed from the infantry. Such an arrangement would have made it unnecessary to call up Cruger's and Allen's corps from Georgia, leaving the troops there to police the interior and perhaps add — marginally — to Brown's at Augusta, where, among other things, they would have provided more support for Col. James Grierson's regiment of royal militia.[31]

Forming mounted troops from the infantry would have been one of the most important ways in which Britain could have met Robson's critique that it was necessary to improvise and adapt to American conditions if the war was to be won. Forming new, fully equipped cavalry corps was not the answer, dependent as they were on cavalry accoutrements shipped from Britain — accoutrements that were expensive, very limited in number, and took months if not years to arrive. What was needed was not carbines, sabres, horse pistols and the rest, but simply getting the infantry with their firelocks mounted that they might meet the revolutionary irregulars on their own terms, given that it was impossible to force them to an engagement with infantry only. Equipped with horses and Pennsylvanian rifles alone, the revolutionary irregulars gave ample evidence of what a formidable force mounted infantry solely equipped with firelocks might be.

Yet a sufficiency of troops, many mounted, to police both provinces was only part of the equation. If pacification was to be maintained or ultimately succeed, those of the revolutionary persuasion had to be convinced that the consequences of taking up arms were greater than the alternative of remaining peaceably at home, where they would have to supply only a measure of provisions in lieu of their enrolment in the royal militia. So, inevitably, we come back to the fact that, apart from allowing

---

[31] For a biographical note on Grierson, see CP, 2: 190.

14

them to occupy their property peaceably, pacification ultimately depended on deterrence, first on effectively suppressing outbreaks of resistance, using if necessary the kind of tactics I have outlined, and second on imposing severe sanctions for either taking up arms or breaking paroles or oaths of allegiance — but deterrence would work only if there were sufficient troops to ensure that most transgressors were caught and punished. Of course, whenever a nascent insurgency may develop, there is always a fine line to be drawn between obtaining the desired effect with deterrent measures and going too far with them, thereby provoking the outcome that they were meant to forestall. Yet, all in all, the option of effective deterrence had to be tried here, for there was no other besides lenity, which, as matters soon proved, stood no chance of success. As Robson aptly remarked of British strategy throughout the war, "The results of following the conciliatory point of view were generally disastrous."[32]

What, then, were the severe sanctions available to the British? Short of using corporal punishment more widely, they were in fact few. In the absence of more prison ships — in any event only a temporary expedient, long-term imprisonment was not an option, for the Provost in Charlestown was overflowing as were the small jails at Orangeburg and Ninety Six. In Georgia the position was even worse. In the case of those who revolted against the reinstatement of the King's peace, but were not subject to paroles or oaths of allegiance, there was a measure available that has had a long pedigree. It was adopted by Major James Wemyss[33], as sanctioned by Cornwallis, when he burned the plantations of those to the east who had taken up arms. I say "a long pedigree" advisedly, for the destruction of homes in like circumstances was, for example, sanctioned by the British in Palestine, where the legislation was kept on the Statute Book by

---

[32] Robson, *American Revolution*, 118.
[33] For a biographical note on Wemyss (pronounced "Weems"), "the second most hated man in South Carolina", see CP, 1: 305.

the State of Israel, which controversially uses it to the present day. Made under article 6 of the Palestine (Defence) Order in Council 1937, regulation 119(1) of the Defence (Emergency) Regulations 1945 says: "A military commander may by order direct the forfeiture to the Government of Palestine of any house, structure or land from which he has reason to suspect that any firearm has been illegally discharged, or any bomb, grenade or explosive or incendiary article illegally thrown, or of any house, structure or land situated in any area, town, village, quarter or street the inhabitants or some of the inhabitants of which he is satisfied have committed, or attempted to commit, or abetted the commission of, or been accessories after the fact of the commission of, any offence against the Regulations involving violence or intimidation or any Military Court offence; and when any house, structure or land is forfeited as aforesaid, the military commander may destroy the house or the structure or anything growing on the land." As for breaking paroles or oaths of allegiance, the sanction of burning plantations remained an option, particularly if transgressors were not apprehended, but if they were, the ultimate sanction, on conviction by court martial, was sentence of death. Yet, as we have seen, such sentences were at times commuted by Cornwallis, lessening their deterrent effect, whereas Germain, the British secretary of state, appeared on the contrary to favour their being generally carried out, seemingly convinced, as he was, of their deterrent value.[34]

If there was one British officer who above all others understood the need for deterrence, it was Lt. Col. Banastre Tarleton, commander of the British Legion. A charismatic leader of men, he gained a deserved reputation for severity in the south and indeed, when we read his letter of 5 August 1780 in which he speaks of fire and confiscation,[35] he may be thought to have damned himself with his own pen. Yet underlying his words is a defensible approach to the war which has received scant

---

[34] See Germain to Cornwallis, 9 November 1780, CP, 3: 45.
[35] CP, 1: 365.

16

attention from American writers, who, apart from Scotti and Piecuch, have superficially and uncritically followed revolutionary propaganda in demonising the man.[36]

Of the factors which formed the backdrop to Tarleton's approach, two predominated. First, inevitably, was the paucity of British, Hessian, and British American troops, as delineated earlier. Second, there was the nature of the war itself, where the constitution and, for those living in North America, one's very sense of national identity were at stake. In such a contest it was unrealistic to assume that committed members of the revolutionary — and indeed the loyalist — party could ever be persuaded to change their views. Dissemble in public they might well be prepared to do, but in their heart of hearts they were as unlikely to forsake their allegiance as to sell it for a mess of pottage.

If we are to draw the correct inferences from Tarleton's *Campaigns*, it was considerations such as these which led him to conclude that the war in the south could not be won by lenity and conciliation. In Tarleton's eyes such a policy, as practised by Cornwallis, would not succeed in winning over the committed. Instead, by minimising the consequences if they were captured, it served only to induce many to take up arms. Apart from the examples previously mentioned, such lenity and its pernicious effect were graphically described by Col. Robert Gray when he reflected on the war in March 1782: "... when the rebel militia were made prisoners, they were immediately delivered up to the regular officers, who, being entirely ignorant of the dispositions and manners of the people, treated them with the utmost lenity and sent them home to their plantations upon parole; and in short, they were treated in every respect as foreign enemies.

---

[36] Anthony J Scotti Jr, *Brutal Virtue: The Myth and Reality of Banastre Tarleton* (Westminster MD: Heritage Books, 2007); Jim Piecuch, *The Blood Be Upon Your Head: Tarleton and the Myth of Buford's Massacre* (Lugoff SC: Southern Campaigns of the American Revolution Press, 2010).

The general consequences of this was that they no sooner got out of our hands than they broke their paroles, took up arms, and made it a point to murder every militia man of ours who had any concern in making them prisoners." Gray contrasted British policy with that of the revolutionaries, who, having a better understanding of what was in part a civil war, treated their royal militia captives with severity: "... when ever a militia man of ours was made a prisoner, he was delivered, not to the Continentals, but to the rebel militia, who looked upon him as a State prisoner, as a man who deserved a halter, and therefore treated him with the greatest cruelty."[37]

Like the revolutionaries, Tarleton understood that it was quite useless to try and reconcile political differences in a conflict in which they were so acute. As he might well have said, "A leopard cannot change his spots." In such a polarised situation he, like them, had an intuitive conviction that a winning policy had no option but to rely primarily on deterrence. Indeed, as he saw it, the greater the deterrence, the sooner the restoration of peace and good government under the Crown. Accordingly, in his treatment of "malefactors" who disturbed the peace, as in his encounters generally with the enemy, he came down hard, so that, in the words of Clinton's proclamation of 22 May 1780, he might deter "by the terror of example". With so few troops in South Carolina and Georgia it seemed to him the only practical way to keep a lid on dissension there.[38] And as described in my commentary in *The Cornwallis Papers*, it was a policy which had been successfully practised on a much grander and severer scale by North Carolina revolutionaries during the past five years.[39]

As far as South Carolina's white inhabitants were concerned, we should avoid exaggerating the impact of Tarleton's approach. Although no reliable figures are available, perhaps only one

---

[37] Gray, "Observations", 144-5.
[38] His motto might well have been , "Oderint, dum metuant!" — "Let them hate, so long as they fear!" — a saying attributed to Accius (170-*c*. 90 BC).
[39] CP, 1: 153.

third were committed revolutionaries, and of them only those who took up arms and came within Tarleton's sphere of operations were affected. What is clear, however, is that Tarleton had the stomach for the deterrent and necessarily disagreeable measures involved in suppressing the rebellion, whereas Cornwallis had not. The Wickwires rightly conclude, "Cornwallis had no place in a civil war."[40]

Perhaps the reason why Tarleton was so demonised in the revolutionary propaganda of his day was the fear that his approach to the war, if it had been generally adopted by the British high command, might well have afforded the surest means of pacifying the south. Akin in various respects to Lt. Col. Henry "Light Horse Harry" Lee (Pyle's massacre),[41] he has ever since been subjected to double standards by American writers, who, if he had operated on the revolutionary side, would no doubt have lauded him down the generations. As I have asserted in my commentary in *The Cornwallis Papers*, it is high time that the man was reappraised in a sensible way.

So deterrence and the use of an adequate number of troops, suitably adapted to American conditions, were essential, but if pacification was to succeed, a firm grip had also to be taken by Cornwallis on plundering, alienating, as it did, his friends and propelling his enemies to take up arms.

Pacification would have taken a much longer period than Cornwallis was prepared to allow. As I have observed elsewhere, *"Festina lente!"* was the maxim for success.[42] If the

---

[40] Franklin and Mary Wickwire, *Cornwallis: The American Adventure* (Boston: Houghton Mifflin Co, 1970), 173.
[41] While marching to join Cornwallis at Hillsborough in February 1781, Dr John Pyle and his band of unresisting loyalists were inhumanly butchered by Lee's Legion and Andrew Pickens' men. The event took place near the Haw River, North Carolina (Joseph Graham, "Narrative", in William Henry Hoyt ed., *The Papers of Archibald D Murphey* (Raleigh: Publications of the North Carolina Historical Commission, 1914), 2: 273-6).
[42] *"Festina lente!"* — "Make haste slowly!" (Suetonius, *Augustus*, 25); CP, 2: 32; see also Piers Mackesy, *Could the British have won the War of Independence?* (Worcester MA: Clark University Press, 1976), 19.

measures I have outlined had been implemented, there seems a reasonable prospect that South Carolina and Georgia would have been eventually restored to the King's peace in reality as well as in name, perhaps with the reinstatement of South Carolina's constitution as favoured by Germain. Only then should thoughts have turned to pursuing the overall strategy to the northward, but how? Where were the troops to come from? It would have been folly to remove troops from South Carolina and Georgia, opening the door to the breaking out of an insurgency there, and none for a time would have been available from New York, assuming Clinton had not taken a material detachment with him when he left the south. The answer would have lain in the troop reinforcements arriving at New York in October 1780 and at Charlestown and New York in June and August 1781, together amounting to 8,500 men.[43] Instead of being frittered away on diversionary expeditions like Brig. Gen. Benedict Arnold's and Major Gen. William Phillips'[44] — expeditions that had no effect whatever on the overall strategy of moving northwards from the south, they could have been consolidated for the invasion of North Carolina.

In a convincing memorandum of extraordinary strategic significance, one entirely overlooked by historians, Hector MacAlester explains why the invasion of North Carolina should be mounted, not from the south, which would not solve the problem of maintaining the troops in the back parts, but from the north — from bases in Petersburg and Halifax, which would not only obviate that problem but force the Continental southern army to withdraw lest it be caught in a pincer movement.[45]

As to Virginia, it would remain, at least for the time being, a bridge too far.[46]

---

[43] References to the reinforcements, their numbers, and places of arrival may be found in Clinton, *The American Rebellion*, 219; and CP, 3: 38, 5: 297-8, and 6: 24.
[44] Those to Virginia in December 1780 and March 1781.
[45] CP, 4: 138-9. For a biographical note on MacAlester, see ibid., 139.
[46] In another compelling plan (CP, 6: 206-8) Hector MacAlester explains how a conquest of Virginia may be put in train. The troops should not of course have

So how do I envisage the war ending? Well, as Clausewitz pertinently put it, "Not every war need be fought till one side collapses ... in war many roads lead to success and they do not all involve the opponent's outright defeat" — the most important of these being to wear the enemy down.[47] With North Carolina conquered, Virginia threatened next, and France and Spain vacillating about a continuance of the war, there was a reasonable prospect that the remaining colonies would have accepted an accommodation short of independence, one giving them all they had sought before hostilities commenced. So, responding to the question posed in the title of this essay, I conclude — like Mackesy, but for wider reasons — that the answer was "Yes".[48]

∞ — ∞

come from those invading North Carolina or possessing the provinces to its south, which it would remain a folly to remove, but rather from further reinforcements sent out by Britain — a prospect, perhaps not at present, but certain if peace with France and Spain, which was on the cards, were concluded.

[47] Clausewitz, *On War*, 33-7.

[48] Of British historians, Robson and Wright conclude that the war had effectively been lost by the close of 1778, whereas Mackesy takes the view that peace with France and Spain, which was in prospect, would have ultimately led to an end of the war in Britain's favour (Robson, *American Revolution*, 114; Esmond Wright, *Fabric of Freedom 1763-1800* (London: Macmillan & Co Ltd, 1965), 128; Mackesy, *Could the British have won?* 23-4, 28). I on the other hand explicitly explain how the end may have come about.

∞ 2 ∞

The Revolutionary War In The South: Re-Evaluations Of Certain Actors And Events

Prefatory remarks

Wide-ranging and to some degree disparate as they are, my re-evaluations are, on the one hand, compartmentalised under the sub-headings set out below and, on the other, placed in the context of the historiography relating to them. Based preponderantly on *The Cornwallis Papers*,[1] they crystallise my reassessment of the persons and events addressed.

As ever, when it comes to the historiography of the southern campaigns, it is a question of separating the wheat from the chaff. On Major Gen. Nathanael Greene alone, the Continental GOC in the south, five works were published between 1960 and 1972, and since then the rate of publication has increased, particularly in recent years.[2] Yet apart from Thayer's and Treacy's scholarly

---

[1] Ian Saberton ed:, *The Cornwallis Papers: The Campaigns of 1780 and 1781 in the Southern Theatre of the American Revolutionary War*, 6 vols (Uckfield: The Naval & Military Press Ltd, 2010) ("CP").

[2] Theodore Thayer, *Nathanael Greene: Strategist of the American Revolution* (New York: Twayne Publishers, 1960); M. F. Treacy, *Prelude to Yorktown: The Southern Campaign of Nathanael Greene, 1780-1781* (Chapel Hill: University of North Carolina Press, 1963); Clifford L. Alderman, *Retreat to Victory: The Life of Nathanael Greene* (Philadelphia: Chilton Book Co, 1967); Ralph Edgar Bailey, *Guns over the Carolinas: The Story of Nathanael Greene* (New York: William Morrow, 1967); Elswyth Thane, *The Fighting Quaker: Nathanael Greene* (New York: Hawthorn Books, 1972); Richard K. Showman, Dennis M. Conrad, Roger N. Parks, et al. eds, *The Papers of General Nathanael Greene*, vols VI to IX (Chapel Hill: University of North Carolina Press, 1991-97); Gregory D. Massey and Jim Piecuch eds, *General Nathanael Greene and the American Revolution in the South* (Columbia: The University of South Carolina Press, 2012). The many recent

studies on the one hand, Showman's edition of Greene's own papers on the other, and the thought-provoking work edited by Massey and Piecuch, none adds, at least for the military historian, to a better understanding of Greene's character, strategy and tactics. Keeping track of works on Greene is of course a mere microcosm of the picture as a whole. As Cogliano has stated, "The present literature on the American Revolution is so vast that it would be impossible to digest it in a lifetime ... more works pour off the presses monthly."[3] There, historiographically, lies the rub.

Overall, I remain of opinion that militarily the broad picture of the war as portrayed by American historians has not markedly altered since the 1970s, but almost all of their interpretive works are written from a perspective that does not coincide with my aim to provide an accurate, balanced and dispassionate commentary on the war. *Ipso facto*, I have — whether here or elsewhere — preferred to base my own conclusions mostly on primary and secondary material rather than on the reworking or interpretation of it in tertiary form, even though in some respects there is a measure of agreement between the latter and myself.[4]

---

biographies of Greene include Lee Patrick Anderson, *Forgotten Patriot: The Life and Times of Major-General Nathanael Greene* (Boca Raton, FL: Universal Publishers, 2002); Gerald M. Carbone, *Nathanael Greene: A Biography of the American Revolution* (London and New York: Palgrave Macmillan, 2008); Terry Golway, *Washington's General: Nathanael Greene and the Triumph of the American Revolution* (New York: Henry Holt & Co, 2005); Steven E. Siry, *Greene: Revolutionary General* (Lincoln, Nebr: Potomac Books, 2007); Spencer C. Tucker, *Rise and Fight Again: The Life of Nathanael Greene* (Wilmington: Intercollegiate Studies Institute, 2009).

[3] Francis D. Cogliano, *Revolutionary America 1763-1815: A political history* (Abingdon: Routledge, 2000), 2.

[4] I use "secondary" to describe material emanating from interviews or conversations with persons who had taken part in, or lived through, the war. By "tertiary" I mean material that is neither primary nor secondary and, to the extent that it relies on other tertiary material, needs to be treated with a measure of caution.

Re-evaluations of certain British
or British American actors

Sir Henry Clinton

Much has been written about Clinton's character, whether, for example, by Willcox, Willcox and Wyatt, or more recently O'Shaughnessy, but none in so many words draws the fundamental conclusion that I do.[5] For instance Willcox and Wyatt, who in their psychological exploration of Clinton's character dwell equally on the problems of a diagnostic approach based on limited historical evidence, conclude that the paradoxes of his conduct can largely be explained by the assumption that he suffered from a conflict, unresolved since childhood, between craving and dreading to exercise authority. "The central point is that Clinton, although greedy for authority, was afraid of exercising it because it represented an area, the paternal, where a part of himself insisted he did not belong ... This conflict affected both phases of his American career. When he was intent on telling his superiors what to do, he obviously craved power ... As commander in chief, responsible only to the distant ministers of the Crown, he was hesitant and unhappy about using his power; his attitude suggests an unconscious conviction that he ought not to have it."[6]

I on the other hand come to what appears to me a simpler, more commonplace conclusion that Clinton exhibited the classic

---

[5] Sir Henry Clinton, *The American Rebellion*, edited by William B. Willcox (New Haven: Yale University Press, 1954),, ix-li; William B. Willcox and Frederick Wyatt, "Sir Henry Clinton: A Psychological Exploration in History," *William and Mary Quarterly*, 3rd ser., 16, No. 1 (January, 1959), 3-26; William B. Willcox, *Portrait of a General: Sir Henry Clinton in the War of Independence* (New York: Alfred A Knopf, 1964), ch. XII; idem, "Sir Henry Clinton: Paralysis of Command," in George Athan Billias ed., *George Washington's Generals and Opponents: Their Exploits and Leadership* (Boston, MA: Da Capo Press, 1994), 2: 73-102; Andrew O'Shaughnessy, "'The Scapegoat': Sir Henry Clinton," in his *The Men Who Lost America: British Command during the Revolutionary War and the Preservation of the Empire* (London: Oneworld Publications, 2013), 214.
[6] Willcox and Wyatt, "Sir Henry Clinton," 12, 17-19.

signs of someone suffering from a marked sense of inadequacy, a conclusion that implicitly reflects on his entire conduct of the war.[7] No such link is explicitly drawn in any of Willcox's cited works. As to the principal signs exhibited by Clinton, he, as a subordinate, was overassertive, overcritical, and overly resentful when his advice was rejected; he, as commander-in-chief, was prickly, belittling of his colleagues, and quick to assume they were incompetent; he stored up perceived grievances aplenty; and typically, when associated with his other traits, he was shy, diffident, and did not mingle easily.

Banastre Tarleton

The *bête noir* of the southern campaigns, Lt. Col. Banastre Tarleton, commander of the British Legion, has received an almost uniformly bad press in America, being castigated for severity in a tide of vilification that began during the Revolution and continues to the present day. Yet underlying his actions, as I have sought in my first essay to maintain, was a defensible approach to the war which has received scant attention from American writers, who, apart from the two notable exceptions below, have superficially and uncritically followed revolution-ary propaganda in demonising the man. In a nutshell, his sever-ity, like that of the revolutionaries, was grounded on "an intuitive conviction that a winning policy had no option but to rely primarily on deterrence. Indeed, as he saw it, the greater the deterrence, the sooner the restoration of peace and good gov-ernment under the Crown."

My reappraisal of Tarleton is in part a contribution to an ongoing academic debate about him that began with the publication of two works by Scotti and Piecuch in 2007 and 2010. Scotti maintains that "there is no real quantitative or qualitative evidence that suggests his men committed more depredations than anyone else in the Revolutionary War." He later goes on,

---

[7] CP, 1: 6.

"In the process [*of mythologising the man, as continued by modern historians,*] Americans have divorced themselves from the reality, which is that Banastre Tarleton is no more guilty or innocent of wanton devastation than anyone else who participated in that struggle." Piecuch, for his part, questions whether Tarleton and his men were ever guilty of a deliberate massacre at the Waxhaws.[8]

Among those eminent British historians who have written about the Revolution since World War II, Mackesy, Robson and Wright have made no criticism of Tarleton. Indeed Wright remarks, "Of the British tactical commanders, there were two ... who were both clever and positive, now deeply buried though they are in the seventh circle of execration in America: Arnold and Tarleton." He later continues, "Whatever his relationship with Mary (Perdita) Robinson, who helped him write his book on the war as well as his parliamentary speeches, and whom, true to his lights, he deserted, Tarleton showed an energy and capacity all too rare among the British commanders. To Rochambeau, however, as to all Americans, he was 'a butcher and a barbarian'."[9]

Nisbet Balfour

Lt. Col. Nisbet Balfour fared for many years little better than Tarleton in the eyes of American historians. A son of the Laird of Dunbog in the County of Fife, he was born in 1743 and by the summer of 1780 had been commanding the Royal Welch Fusiliers for two and a half years.

As British occupation of South Carolina's backcountry began, he was seconded to the command of Ninety Six but would

---

[8] Anthony J. Scotti Jr., *Brutal Virtue: The Myth and Reality of Banastre Tarleton* (Westminster MD: Heritage Books, 2007), 135 and 137; Jim Piecuch, *The Blood Be Upon Your Head: Tarleton and the Myth of Buford's Massacre* (Lugoff, SC: Southern Campaigns of the American Revolution Press, 2010), 27-40.
[9] Esmond Wright, *Fabric of Freedom 1763-1800* (London; Macmillan & Co Ltd, 1965), 117.

not remain there for long. Cornwallis would soon appoint him Commandant of Charlestown in place of Brig. Gen. James Paterson, who on 18 July 1780 was conveniently shipped off to New York for the recovery of his health.[10] It was an exemplary appointment. Arriving in Charlestown at the beginning of August, Balfour at once applied himself efficiently and indefatigably to the job, which involved not only managing the very complex civil affairs of the town and country but also supporting militarily the troops in the field. An imposing figure, he is accurately described as being "altogether a very fine specimen of physical manhood, with an erect person fully six feet in height, broad-chested and athletic, with cheeks unwrinkled, a skin clear and florid, eyes large, blue and tolerably expressive, and features generally well-chiselled." In the uniform of his regiment he was, in the words of a lady who knew him well, "as splendid as scarlet, gold lace and feathers could make a man."

Occupying as headquarters a mansion at No. 11 Lower King Street belonging to the estate of Miles Brewton, Balfour soon began to ruffle the feathers of revolutionary Charlestonians. According to David Ramsay, a leading incendiary who, having been a member of the revolutionary legislature, was transported to St. Augustine for breaking his parole, he displayed in the exercise of his office "the frivolous self-importance, and all the disgusting insolence, which are natural to little minds when puffed up by sudden elevation and employed in functions to which their abilities are not equal." In particular Ramsay objected to Balfour and his assistants exercising legislative, judicial and executive powers over citizens in the same manner as over the common soldiery under their command. For his part Brig. Gen. William Moultrie, who commanded the revolutionary prisoners, accused Balfour of "violent and arbitrary administration," asserting that "Balfour, a proud, haughty Scot, carried his authority with a very high hand. His tyrannical, insolent disposition treated the people as the most abject slaves." [11]

---

[10] For a biographical note on Paterson, see CP, 1: 49.
[11] David Ramsay, *The History of the Revolution of South-Carolina from a British Province to an Independent State*, (Trenton, 1785), 2: 263-4; William Moultrie,

Of Balfour's critics Ramsay was the first to go into print, merely two years after the close of the war. It was he who set the tone for American writing about the military history of the war for well over a century. Despite stating that he had endeavoured "to write impartially for the good of mankind," he has provided a wonderfully unbalanced, tendentious version of events laced with partisan vituperation, as in the case of Balfour. Others, for example Lee, Lossing and McCrady, have followed suit with equally damning remarks.[12]

Fortunately for Balfour the passage of time has led to a less emotive and more balanced assessment of his conduct. Like Cornwallis, he was faced with the realities of power. In the situation in which he found himself he had inevitably no option but to adopt measures which were designed forcibly and inescapably to put down rebellion. This being so, it was only natural for the revolutionary party to consider those measures oppressive. Indeed, they cannot have been otherwise if the aim was eventually to reinstate civil government under the Crown. As the saying goes, you cannot make an omelette without breaking eggs.

Extraordinarily preoccupied with the heavy duties of his office, Balfour personally had little time for those incorrigible revolutionaries who persevered at times in trying to score points. Rather short with them he may have been, but his arduous responsibilities did not allow him the freedom to be otherwise. Politically, they were beyond redemption.

Of latter-day American historians McCowen to some degree shares my assessment of Balfour, asserting that "little

---

Memoirs of the American Revolution (New York, 1802), 300. For a biographical note on Moultrie, see CP, 1: 373-4.

[12] Henry Lee, *Memoirs of the War in the Southern Department of the United States* (revised edition, New York, 1869), 462; Benson J. Lossing, *The Pictorial Field-Book of the Revolution*, 2 vols (New York, 1855), 2: 568n; Edward McCrady, *The History of South Carolina in the Revolution 1775-1780* (New York: The Macmillan Co, 1901), 715.

can be found to substantiate the accusations of Moultrie and Ramsay," to which I have referred. He continues, "As British commandant, Balfour was understandably unyielding toward the revolutionaries. He scrupulously carried out the commands of his superiors in regard to policies in Charleston and wisely deferred to the Board of Police in civil matters. Thus there would seem to be little reason to regard Balfour as the villain of the British occupation of Charleston. Perhaps Moultrie and Ramsay were too personally involved in the events of the time to evaluate objectively the effectiveness of the British officer whose personality they found overbearing."[13]

As revealed in *The Cornwallis Papers*, Balfour's immense contribution to the British war effort in the Carolinas speaks for itself. Always an entertaining writer, he comes across as an officer who never shirked responsibility but rather took it upon himself, an officer never loath to take the tough decision. Right, for example, in promoting the transportation of incendiaries to St. Augustine, undoubtedly right in confirming the sentence of death on Col. Isaac Hayne, he may, for example, be criticised for closely confining Continental and militia captives on prison ships, a decision which led many to die of small pox or putrid fevers. Yet taken together, his decisions were invariably sound in furthering the interests of the Crown.[14]

If Balfour was more commonly fallible, it was in his assessment of subordinate officers. While right to a degree about the impetuosity of Major Patrick Ferguson, the Inspector of Militia, he was, for example, quite wrong in criticising Lt. Col. John Harris Cruger for lack of confidence, an officer whose sterling qualities were amply displayed in the siege of Ninety Six. Devoted to Cornwallis, he only once came close to regretting his judgement, namely to march from Wilmington into Virginia.[15]

---

[13] George Smith McCowen Jr., *The British Occupation of Charleston, 1780-82* (Columbia: University of South Carolina Press, 1972), 144-5.
[14] For a biographical note on Hayne, see CP, 6: 78.
[15] For a biographical note on Cruger, see CP, 1: 152, and 258.

After the war Balfour was rewarded by promotion to colonel and by appointment as an aide-de-camp to the King. He went on to become an MP and see service as a major general in Flanders. Unmarried, he died a full general at Dunbog in 1823.

John Watson Tadwell Watson

Watson was the lieutenant colonel commanding a corps of British American light infantry that arrived at Charlestown in mid December 1780. Much has been written, whether by revolutionary participants or later, about his brief service in South Carolina, particularly his fraught expedition to the east and his encounters with Brig. Gen. Francis Marion, but how he came to be serving there instead of taking part in the winter campaign, what was his character as a Guards officer, and why he failed to reinforce Col. Francis Lord Rawdon before the Battle of Hobkirk's Hill have remained a mystery.[16]

Drawing on *The Cornwallis Papers*, I conclude that he was typical of many a Guards officer down the years, seemingly puffed up with self-importance and reluctant to obey or cooperate with

---

[16] See, for example, William Dobein James, *A Sketch of the Life of Brig. Gen. Francis Marion and A History of His Brigade* (Charleston, 1821), *passim*; William Johnson, *Sketches of the Life and Correspondence of Nathanael Greene, Major General of the Armies of the United States*, (Charleston, 1822), 2: 68, 71-2, 104-5; Robert W. Gibbes ed., *Documentary History of the American Revolution consisting of Letters and Papers relating to the Contest for Liberty, chiefly in South Carolina*, (Columbia, SC, 1853), iii, *passim*; Lossing, *Field-Book*, 2: 472-75, 479, 500-01, 565-66; David Duncan Wallace, *South Carolina: A Short History, 1520-1948* (reprint of 1951 edition, Columbia: University of South Carolina Press, 1969), 315; Mark Mayo Boatner III, *Encyclopedia of the American Revolution* (New York: David McKay Co, 1973), 1172; Robert D. Bass, *Swamp Fox: The Life and Campaigns of General Francis Marion* (reprint of 1959 edition, Columbia: The Sandlapper Press Inc, 1976), *passim*; Hugh F Rankin, *Francis Marion: The Swamp Fox* (New York: Thomas Y Crowell Company, 1973), *passim*; Showman et al. eds, *The Greene Papers*, vols VII and VIII, *passim*; John Buchanan, *The Road to Guilford Courthouse: The American Revolution in the Carolinas* (New York: John Wiley and Sons Inc, 1997), 395-6; John W. Gordon, *South Carolina and the American Revolution: A Battlefield History* (Columbia: University of South Carolina Press, 2003), 142. For a biographical note on Rawdon, see CP, 1: 151-2.

ranking officers such as Rawdon, Balfour and Tarleton whom he considered his professional inferiors. It was for this reason that Cornwallis decided not to take him and his men on the winter campaign because there would have been a constant difficulty of command between him and Tarleton. As regards his failure to reinforce Rawdon, he may have disobeyed orders, they may have miscarried, or he may have been unavoidably delayed by Balfour's stopping him to cover the ferries for Cornwallis's possible return from Wilmington.[17]

Alexander Stewart and Paston Gould

The basics of Stewart's service in the south have long been known. Born in 1739 and a native of Ayrshire, he was lieutenant colonel of the 3rd Regiment (the Buffs) and had arrived with it at Charlestown in early June 1781 as part of a reinforcement from Ireland commanded by Col. Paston Gould. In early July he would lead his regiment to a junction with Rawdon at Orangeburg, where Rawdon, who was returning on sick leave to England, handed over to him command of the troops on the frontier. On 8 September he led them bravely in the Battle of Eutaw Springs.

So much for his service, but what of his character, about which history has remained silent? Fortunately the *The Cornwallis Papers* includes certain facts about him and allows certain conclusions to be drawn, none of which portrays him in an entirely creditable light. Admittedly beset with personal problems of a financial nature, he comes across as a forceful personality overly preoccupied with rank, advancement, and reward — as one who in his letters to Cornwallis is not averse to leaning on their past acquaintance to try and obtain preferment. Had these preoccupations not affected the conduct of the King's service, then all would have been well, but on at least one occasion they did. In a damning letter of 7 June Rawdon

---

[17] For a biographical note on Watson, see CP, 2: 199-200.

explains to Cornwallis how and why Stewart influenced Gould "to run rusty" by refusing to cooperate in the attempt to relieve Ninety Six. It was left almost entirely to the exertions of Rawdon and Balfour that the successful attempt was made. For his part Cornwallis plainly understood the nature of the creature with whom he was dealing, as may be read between the lines of his letter to Stewart of 16 July.[18]

In December 1781 Stewart would achieve his cherished promotion to brigadier general and in 1782-3 serve in Jamaica. In 1786 he entered the Commons as the Member for Kircudbright Stewartry, a seat he would hold till his death in 1794. Four years earlier he had been promoted to major general.

The character of Gould also remained a mystery. The titular successor to Rawdon, he was, as I conclude from *The Cornwallis Papers*, a weak man, a previously unrevealed consideration that led Cornwallis to supersede him with Major Gen. Alexander Leslie. Blame for not cooperating in the relief of Ninety Six must also be laid at his door.[19]

Patrick Ferguson

A consensus has yet to arise as to Ferguson's character as Inspector of Militia, though *The Cornwallis Papers* goes a long way to supporting my own overall conclusion that he was a humane, benevolent officer who, despite trying circumstances, applied his best endeavours to discipline the royal militia and suppress their irregularities. Yet unsubstantiated criticism continues to creep out of the woodwork — and from surprising quarters. For example Higginbotham, who with Shy has perhaps done most to contribute in recent times to a reassessment of the nature of the war, begins by stating more or less accurately that "the King's friends in the south favored anything but

---

[18] CP, 5: 292, 295, 299 and 6: 169-70.
[19] CP, 5: 292, 294 and 6: 62.

pacification as that word is currently used. Instead they wanted a course of harsh retribution." So far so good, but he then mistakenly contends, at least as far as Ferguson is concerned, that "their views were shared by some of Clinton's subordinates, especially those most exposed to tory opinions such as Banastre Tarleton, Patrick Ferguson, and Lord Rawdon."[20]

It is true that Ferguson had vacillated between favouring a scorched-earth policy and a conciliatory approach to the war, but by 1780 he had come down firmly in support of the latter. Nevertheless, Shy maintains that he remained among the group of "hotheaded young officers ... that advocated the use of fire and sword to defeat the American rebellion."[21]

Thomas Fraser

How Fraser came effectively to command the South Carolina Royalist Regiment in the field has to some extent remained unchartered.

Born in 1755, Fraser was a Scot who had settled before the war in New Jersey. Commissioned a lieutenant in the New York Volunteers in August 1777, he had acted as its adjutant and then as quartermaster.

As his service in the south began, he was seconded as quartermaster to Balfour's detachment on its way to occupy Ninety

---

[20] CP, 1: 38; Don Higginbotham, "Reflections on the War of Independence, Modern Guerrilla Warfare, and the War in Vietnam," in Ronald Hoffman and Peter J. Albert eds., *Arms and Independence: The Military Character of the American Revolution* (Charlottesville: University Press of Virginia, 1984), 20.
[21] Ferguson to Clinton, October 10 and 15, 1778, PRO 5/96(177) and (179) (Kew: UK National Archives); Stephen Conway, "To Subdue America: British Army Officers and the Conduct of the Revolutionary War," *William and Mary Quarterly*, 3rd ser., 43, No. 3 (July, 1986), 383; John Shy, "British Strategy for Pacifying the Southern Colonies, 1778-1781," in Jeffrey J. Crow and Larry E. Tise eds, *The Southern Experience in the American Revolution* (Chapel Hill: University of North Carolina Press, 1978), 167.

Six. A spirited and able officer, he would, as recommended by Balfour, receive a warrant from Cornwallis to raise a company of which he was appointed captain. He proceeded to take part on 19 August 1780 in the action at Musgrove's Mill, where he was wounded. Shortly afterwards Cornwallis appointed him to the majority in the South Carolina Royalist Regiment, backdated to 10 August. With the recall soon after of his commanding officer, Lt. Col. Alexander Innes, first to Charlestown and then to New York, Fraser would take command of the corps in the field and play with it an active part in operations in South Carolina, a part outlined to some extent in *The Cornwallis Papers*.[22]

When the regiment was disbanded at the close of the war, he was placed on the Provincial half-pay list and retired to South Carolina. Marrying there, he engaged at first in the lumber business, establishing saw mills on the Edisto River, but did not appear to prosper. He then became a factor or commission merchant in Charleston. Until his death he continued to receive half pay, and his widow was granted a pension by the Crown.[23]

George Hanger

Hanger played a short but important part in the southern campaigns, being major and second in command of Tarleton's British Legion during the summer and autumn of 1780. As such he made a significant contribution to the victory at Camden and commanded the British van on the entry into Charlotte. It is, however, as author of *An Address to the Army*, one of the relatively few commentaries on the southern campaigns by a British participant, that he is best remembered as far as the war is concerned, a contribution that has led in part to my deciding to write a biography of him. As to his service in America, it corrects manifold inaccuracies littering the historical record.[24]

---

[22] For a biographical note on Innes, see CP, 1: 17.

[23] CP, 1: 243.

[24] The Hon. George Hanger, *An Address to the Army in reply to Strictures of Roderick M'Kenzie (late Lieutenant in the 71st Regiment) on Tarleton's History of the*

James Dunlap

By no means rosy is the picture of Dunlap emanating from revolutionary sources and followed by American historians to this day, but is it accurate? I suspect not.

A captain in the Queen's Rangers on secondment to Ferguson's corps, Dunlap was vilified by the revolutionaries for severity, but scarce one concrete example has come to light, which alone is suspicious.[25] Among recent American historians who have relied on those revolutionary sources are Waring and Bass. Paraphrasing them, but like them in only general terms, Bass remarks, "James Dunlap had been vicious and wanton. His plundering, depredations and murders had aroused uncontrollable hatred."[26]

So, if the historical record is flawed, what do we actually know of Dunlap's service and what reasonable conclusions about his conduct does a re-evaluation lead us to draw? Undoubtedly he played an important part in the operations in South Carolina's backcountry and the adjoining border region. While seeking to promote Ferguson's plan of campaign, he was involved in the actions at Earle's Ford on 15 July 1780, Cedar Spring on 8 August, and Cane Creek on 12 September, where he was severely wounded in the leg. As he recuperated at Gilbertown, a failed attempt was made to murder him in which he was shot in the body. Recovering by early November, he was promoted to major of an irregular corps of horse to be raised in the District of Ninety Six. While foraging with seventy-six of his men on 24

Campaigns of 1780 and 1781 (London, 1789); Ian Saberton, *George Hanger: The Life and Times of an Eccentric Nobleman* (Tolworth: Gloucester House Publishing, 2018).

[25] See, for example, Hugh McCall, *The History of Georgia*, (Savannah, 1816), 2: 352; Johnson, *Greene*, 2: 107; Lyman C. Draper, *King's Mountain and its Heroes* (Cincinnati, 1881), 159 and 164.

[26] Alice N. Waring, *The Fighting Elder: Andrew Pickens (1739-1817)* (University of South Carolina Press, 1962), 41 and 68; Robert D. Bass, *Ninety Six: The Struggle for the South Carolina Back Country* (The Sandlapper Store Inc, 1978), 349.

March 1781, he was attacked at Beattie's Mill on Little River and surrendered after stiff resistance. On his way to Virginia as a prisoner he had got as far as Gilbertown when he was shot and killed in cold blood by a set of men with the connivance of his guard.

Accepted by all as an active, spirited officer, Dunlap has had his drive and determination vilified by revolutionaries as severity — a highly suspicious charge as such conduct would have been so contrary to the humane, conciliatory policy followed by his commanding officer, Ferguson. Accused by revolutionaries of raiding Col. Andrew Pickens' plantation and causing him to break his parole in late December, he was in fact in Charlestown in November and early December before being engaged at the village of Ninety Six in forming his corps of horse. He had still not done so by mid January. Entrusted with this task, he had neither men nor opportunity to trouble Pickens, a course so at odds with British policy to conciliate that man of influence.

It is a peculiar fact of civil wars that adherents of one party tend to blackguard those of the other more bitterly than is common in other forms of warfare. As I have observed elsewhere, there are, despite the passage of years, distinct parallels to be drawn between the Revolutionary War in America and the troubles in Northern Ireland, not least in the attitudes of the opposing sides.[27] Yes, there were occasional lapses by the security forces in Northern Ireland, but an abiding recollection of my service there was the opposing party's unremitting depiction of the security forces' actions in the worst possible light. So, I conclude, was it the case with Dunlap.

Re-evaluations of certain revolutionary actors

Thomas Sumter

While adverting to the internecine warfare waged in the backcountry of South Carolina, the two standard biographies of

---

[27] See CP, 1: back cover.

Thomas Sumter, the brigadier general commanding the revolutionary militia there, gloss over his responsibility for the often barbarous conduct of his men.[28] I do not, although I accept that he was fighting a partisan war. Overall, I assert in *The Cornwallis Papers* that he consistently displayed a marked streak of ruthlessness which did not scruple to employ measures such as cold-blooded murder on a grand scale.[29] How do I come to this necessarily compressed conclusion? Well, from a variety of primary sources.

For example, when Sumter captured Orangeburg on 11 May 1781, thirteen of the loyalist prisoners were shot in cold blood. On 23 November 1780 Cornwallis, who had no reason to lie to a subordinate, advised Lt. Col. John Harris Cruger that Sumter's men "have been guilty of the most horrid outrages." Not only was Sumter responsible but also Col. Thomas Brandon, Lt. Col. Elijah Clark and others, who, as Cornwallis explained on 3 December 1780 to Clinton, "had different corps plundering the houses and putting to death the well affected inhabitants between Tyger River and Pacolet." Next day he observed to Clinton, "I will not hurt your Excellency's feelings by attempting to describe the shocking tortures and inhuman murders which are every day committed by the enemy, not only on those who have taken part with us, but on many who refuse to join them ... I am very sure that unless some steps are taken [*by the enemy*] to check it, the war in this quarter will become truly savage."[30] On 7 March 1781, when Rawdon, then commanding in the field in South Carolina and Georgia, reported to Cornwallis on Sumter's foray down the Congaree and Santee, he remarked generally on "the savage cruelty of the enemy, who commit the most wanton murders in cold blood upon the friends of Government that fall into their

---

[28] Anne King Gregorie, *Thomas Sumter* (Columbia, SC: R L Bryan Co, 1931), *passim*; Robert D. Bass, *Gamecock: The Life and Times of General Thomas Sumter* (New York: Holt, Rinehart and Winston, 1961), *passim*.
[29] CP, 1: 150.
[30] CP, 3: 25 and 38. For biographical notes on Clark and Brandon, see CP, 1: 257 and 295.

hands." Turning specifically to Sumter, he related that, while blockading Fort Granby, Sumter "summoned by proclamation all the inhabitants to join him, offering to all such as would take part with him a full pardon for their former attachment to us and denouncing penalty of death to all who did not range themselves under his standard by the 23rd of February. To give weight to these threats several persons known to be friendly towards us were inhumanly murdered, tho' unarmed and remaining peaceably at their own houses."[31]

From the examples I have cited it is in my opinion fallacious to believe that Sumter did not condone or approve of the barbarous conduct of his men.

Cornwallis well understood the nature of the creature opposed to him. When Major James Wemyss and his wounded men were captured at Fishdam Ford, Cornwallis immediately assumed that they had been ill treated by Sumter. He was of course mistaken, for Sumter never mistreated captured British or British American troops, but Cornwallis's reaction speaks volumes. Nor could he bring himself to write personally to Sumter about the exchange of John Hutchison, a loyalist prisoner whom it was suspected Sumter was about to hang. Although Cornwallis drafted the letter himself, it was signed by Lt. John Money, his aide-de-camp. By contrast he had no compunction about writing to Major Gen. Horatio Gates, Major Gen. Nathanael Greene and Major Gen. William Smallwood, who were other revolutionary commanders in the south.[32]

---

[31] "Levi Smith's Narrative," *The Royal Gazette* (Charlestown), 13-17 April 1782, reprinted in the *Political Magazine* (London), June 1782, 378; CP, 3: 25, 28, 273, and CP, 4: 47.
[32] CP, 3: 68, 74, and CP, 2: 330-1, 341-2. For biographical notes on Gates, Wemyss (pronounced "Weems"), Money, Smallwood and Greene, see CP, 1: 176 and 305; 2: 45 and 56; and 3: 10.

Andrew Williamson

A Scots immigrant, Andrew Williamson (c. 1725-1786) was the brigadier general commanding the revolutionary militia in the backcountry of South Carolina till shortly after the fall of Charlestown. He then capitulated and ever since his status and role have remained in obscurity. "There hangs a heavy cloud over Williamson's conduct at this time," remarks McCrady, but until my pen portrait of him in *The Cornwallis Papers* no one had convincingly succeeded in explaining it.[33]

Since then an article about him has been penned by Toulmin, but it fails to explain Williamson's conduct in response to the British invasion. Before *The Cornwallis Papers* the only biographical information about him was that briefly set out in three dictionaries. None approaches a satisfactory explanation of his behaviour.[34]

Otherwise we are left with brief, scattered and unexplained references to his taking protection, which he did not, or — far fewer — to his entering into a parole, which he did. Protection, of course, involved swearing allegiance to the Crown.[35]

---

[33] Edward McCrady, *The History of South Carolina in the Revolution 1775-1780* (New York: The Macmillan Co, 1901), 527; CP, 1: 77.

[34] Llewellyn M. Toulmin, "Backcountry Warrior: Brig. Gen. Andrew Williamson," *Journal of Backcountry Studies*, 7, Nos 1 and 2 (Spring and Fall, 2012); *American National Biography* (New York: Oxford University Press, 1999), 23: 521-2; *Dictionary of American Biography* (Scribner's, 1936), 10: 296-7; N. Louise Bailey and Elizabeth I. Cooper, *Biographical Directory of the South Carolina House of Representatives* (Columbia: University of South Carolina Press, 1984), 3: 769-71.

[35] Among those asserting or strongly implying that he took protection are John R. Alden, *The South in the Revolution 1763-1789* (Baton Rouge: Louisiana State University Press, 1957). 242, 272; Bass, *Gamecock*, 207; Boatner, *Encyclopedia*, 1210; Draper, *King's Mountain*, 47, 72; William T. Graves, *Backcountry Revolutionary: James Williams (1740-1780)* (Lugoff, SC: Southern Campaigns of the American Revolution Press, 2012), 151; John W. Gordon, *South Carolina and the American Revolution: A Battlefield History* (Columbia: University of South Carolina Press, 2003), 104; Lossing, *Field-Book*, 2: 506n; Jim Piecuch, *Three*

So what motivated Williamson's conduct? Why was he not sent on parole to the offshore islands, as Cornwallis originally intended, being instead assiduously courted by the British in a vain attempt openly to turn him? Basically because he adopted a duplicitous approach, remaining outwardly true to his revolutionary convictions while covertly acting in the British interest, whether by offering confidential advice, for example on the use of the Cherokees against Georgia insurgents, or by persuading his fellow countrymen not to go off to the enemy. Although his motives are not entirely clear, it seems that he wished to stay peaceably at White Hall, his plantation six miles west of Ninety Six on Hard Labor Creek, there doing whatever little was necessary to achieve that end, rather than to refuse to submit, openly opposing the British in the field, or, having submitted, to refuse to cooperate and face banishment to the offshore islands. Losing heart in the revolutionary struggle, he had, in short, opted for the quiet life.

As matters turned out, increasing disorder in the backcountry would lead him to abandon White Hall by summer 1781 for his plantation in St. Paul's Parish, some seven miles from Charlestown. Here on 5 July 1781 he was captured by revolutionary militia but was promptly rescued, precipitating the Hayne affair. Later, true to his duplicitous nature, and contrary to his parole, he would communicate to Greene useful

---

Peoples, One King: Loyalists, Indians, and Slaves in the Revolutionary South, 1775-1782 (Columbia: University of South Carolina Press, 2008), 210, 274; Toulmin, *supra*, 40; and Wallace, *South Carolina*, 297. Among those maintaining that he entered into a parole are Walter Edgar, *Partisans and Redcoats: The Southern Conflict that Turned the Tide of the American Revolution* (New York: Perennial, 2003), 139; Robert Stansbury Lambert, *South Carolina Loyalists in the American Revolution* (Columbia: University of South Carolina Press, 1987), 160-1; Henry Lumkin, *From Savannah to Yorktown: The American Revolution in the South* (St Paul, Minn: Paragon House, 1981), 1, 248; John S. Pancake, *This Destructive War: The British Campaign in the Carolinas, 1780-1782* (reprint of 1985 edition, Tuscaloosa: University of Alabama Press, 2003), 80-1; and David K. Wilson, *The Southern Strategy: Britain's Conquest of South Carolina and Georgia, 1775-1780* (reprint of 2005 edition, Columbia: University of South Carolina Press, 2008), 262.

information about the Charlestown garrison. In January 1782 his extensive properties were confiscated by act of the revolutionary assembly but none was advertised or sold by the confiscation commissioners. Instead, in 1784, he was quietly amerced and disqualified. Two years later he died, apparently on his plantation near Charlestown.

Andrew Pickens

Colonel of the Long Cane revolutionary militia, Pickens was granted a parole after the fall of Charlestown and remained peaceably at home till the close of 1780. He then proceeded to break his parole, went off with a band of his men to take part in the Battle of Cowpens, and for his part in the victory was promoted to brigadier general of militia by the ousted revolutionary governor, John Rutledge.

Relying on McCall, as does Waring, American writers have consistently maintained that Pickens was a man of honour who quite reasonably considered himself released from his parole as a result of being plundered by James Dunlap, a British American officer. It is not a version of events supported by *The Cornwallis Papers*.[36] Based on evidence there, I conclude that it was a fabrication and have until now left the public at large to form its own view of Pickens' conduct.[37] Revealing my own assessment here, I am of opinion that he was indisputably a most effective officer, but sadly, breaking his word as he did, he was no gentleman.

Besides Waring's, Pickens had been the subject of three other biographies prior to the publication of *The Cornwallis Papers*. Since then one by Reynolds, a direct descendent of Pickens' brother Joseph, has appeared. An academically flawed

---

[36] See "James Dunlap," *supra*.
[37] McCall, *History*, 2: 352; Waring, *The Fighting Elder*, 41-2; CP, 1: 74-5 and 79.

work, it materially lacks balance and is not averse to a cavalier treatment of primary sources. The latest by Andrew is the most authoritative.[38]

Benjamin Cleveland

The picture that has come down to us of Cleveland, colonel of the Wilkes County, North Carolina revolutionary militia, is very much as painted by Draper, who maintains that he was quite justifiably "the terror of terrors" to all Tories but to all others "the jolly 'Old Roundabout' of the Yadkin," a sobriquet derived from the name of his plantation. Examples of a succession of American writers who have followed suit are Landrum, Crouch, Ashe, Hickerson and Russell.[39] I myself on the other hand, based on evidence that Draper himself provides, supplemented by Major Patrick Ferguson's own comments in *The Cornwallis Papers*, suggest that his barbarous conduct was far too excessive and betrayed in him a marked streak of sadism.

So what briefly do we know about Cleveland? Born in Prince William County, Virginia, in 1738, he was taken while very young to a border settlement on Blue Run and by early manhood had developed a keen love of hunting, gaming, horse racing, and the

---

[38] Cecil B. Hartley, *Heroes and Patriots of the South: comprising lives of General Francis Marion, General William Moultrie, General Andrew Pickens, and Governor John Rutledge* (Philadelphia, 1860); Andrew Lee Pickens, *Skyagunsta: the border wizard owl, Major-General Andrew Pickens (1739-1817)* (Greenville, SC: Observer Printing Co, 1934); William Hayne Mills, *The Life of General Andrew Pickens* (Clemson, SC: 1958); William R. Reynolds, *Andrew Pickens: South Carolina Patriot in the Revolutionary War* (Jefferson, NC: McFarland & Co Inc, 2012); Rod Andrew Jr, *The Life and Times of Andrew Pickens: Revolutionary War Hero, American Founder* (Chapel Hill: University of North Carolina Press, 2017).
[39] Draper, *King's Mountain*, 425-54; J. B. O. Landrum, *Colonial and Revolutionary History of Upper South Carolina* (Greenville SC, 1897), 224-29; John Crouch, *Historical Sketches of Wilkes County* (Wilkesboro, NC, 1902), 11-35; Samuel A'Court Ashe, *Biographical History of North Carolina from colonial times to the present* (Greensboro, NC, 1906), 5: 69-73; Thomas Felix Hickerson, *Happy Valley, History and Genealogy* (Chapel Hill: University of North Carolina Press, 1940), 7-9; David Lee Russell, *The American Revolution in the Southern Colonies* (Jefferson, NC: McFarland & Co Inc, 2000), 189; CP, 2: 33 and 135. .

wild frolicking common on the frontier. About 1769 he migrated to Rowan County, North Carolina, settling on the upper Yadkin River. With the onset of the Revolution he became a captain in the revolutionary militia and took park in the Cherokee expedition of 1776. Afflicted with a serious speech impediment and weighing fully eighteen stones, he began to show a darker side to his character when suppressing loyalists and earned a reputation for summary hangings, floggings, and mutilation. By now colonel of the Wilkes County revolutionary militia, he had been appointed a justice of the County Court and had twice been elected to the revolutionary legislature. An inspirational leader, he courageously led his men in the Battle of King's Mountain, but not content with victory, he was conspicuous in bringing about the mock trial and hanging of loyalist prisoners at Bickerstaff's Old Fields, undoubtedly desiring, in keeping with his character, a little light entertainment.

After the war he moved to the Tugaloo region of western South Carolina, where he served for many years as a justice of the Pendleton (now Oconee) County Court. As a judge he had great contempt for technicalities and for the arguments of lawyers, often sleeping on the bench. At his death in 1806 he weighed over thirty-two stones.[40]

Thomas Polk

Having previously served as colonel of the 4th North Carolina Continental Regiment, Polk went on to become the commissary in charge of supplying both the North Carolina and southern Continental forces in 1780. While otherwise relating well known facts about him, I tread new ground in The Cornwallis Papers by drawing on evidence there to suggest that he had in mind becoming a traitor to the revolutionary cause.[41]

Although Polk is described in the Dictionary of American Biography as "a zealous patriot," other works have pointed out

---

[40] CP, 2: 135.
[41] Ibid., 115.

that Gates considered his conduct suspicious at this time, but no concrete evidence has been forthcoming, and certainly none as damning as that set out in *The Cornwallis Papers*.[42]

Re-evaluations of certain events

Clinton's proclamation of 3 June 1780

This proclamation has been oft and uniformly interpreted as forcing the disaffected in South Carolina to choose between supporting the Crown or taking up arms against it.

Yes, it cancelled the paroles of those not in the military line, but as interpreted by Cornwallis, it did not cancel the paroles of those who had served in the revolutionary forces during the British operations in South Carolina. Of the disaffected to whom the proclamation applied, we see from *The Cornwallis Papers* that none were to be permitted to enter the royal militia, so that none were to be required to take up arms against their fellow revolutionaries. Instead, having been disarmed, they were to be allowed to remain at home, being required only to contribute a measure of supplies in lieu of their personal attendance in the militia. *Ipso facto*, the notion that the proclamation in itself precipitated the disaffected into choosing between fighting for the British or fighting for the enemy is patently false.[43]

The damage was in fact done, not by the proclamation and the eminently reasonable way in which it was applied by Cornwallis, but rather by the gloss placed on it by militant revolutionaries, who, though relatively few, propagated a most deceitful and persuasive interpretation of its effect, an interpretation which

---

[42] See, for example, Lossing, *Field-Book*, 418; John Hill Wheeler, *Reminiscences and Memoirs of North Carolina and Eminent North Carolinians* (reprint, Baltimore, MD: Genealogical Publishing Co, 1966), 282; Blackwell P. Robinson, *William R. Davie* (Chapel Hill: University of North Carolina Press, 1957), 96; Showman et al. eds, *The Greene Papers*, 6: 559n.

[43] Cornwallis's general plan for regulating South Carolina and his dispatch of 30 June 30 1780 to Clinton support my own interpretation, CP, 1: 123-4 and 160-1.

has gained uncritical acceptance down the years. As Lt. Col. George Turnbull observed, when citing another instance of revolutionary propaganda, "It is inconceivable the damage such reports has done."[44]

Besides misrepresentation of British policy, another reason for becoming actively disaffected may have been plundering by "men cloathed in green" — presumably British Legion cavalrymen, who were notorious for it — and by loyalists, or settlers professing to be loyalists. However, many of those soon to take up arms would require no such reasons and, if subject to paroles or protections, would be unconcerned about the niceties of observing them. Once the shock of the occupation had passed, some, committed as they were to the Revolution, and others, influenced or intimidated by the committed into supporting it, would quite simply take up arms in its defence.

The action at the Waxhaws, 29 May 1780

No matter Piecuch's contention that no deliberate massacre took place at the Waxhaws, the vast disparity in the number of casualties alone suggests that a disreputable bloodbath occurred — a fact that Lt. Col. Banastre Tarleton himself, in so many words, admits, as does Charles Stedman, a commissary serving with Cornwallis. Various American historians have maintained, ever since the close of the war, that Tarleton was responsible for ordering the slaughter, but was he, and did the action instigate, as is generally asserted, the merciless barbarity with which the war was waged by the revolutionary irregulars and state troops?[45]

---

[44] CP, 1: 139. For a biographical note on Turnbull, see ibid., 138.

[45] Piecuch, *The Blood Be Upon Your Head*, 27-40; Banastre Tarleton, *A History of the Campaigns of 1780 and 1781 in the Southern Provinces of North America* (London, 1787), 31; Charles Stedman, *History of the Origin, Progress, and Termination of the American War* (London, 1792), 2: 193, 325. For American accounts down the years of Tarleton's involvement see, for example, Ramsay, *History*, 2: 109-10; James, *Marion*, Appendix, 1-7; Joseph Johnson, *Traditions and Reminiscences chiefly of the American Revolution in the South* (Charleston, 1851),

In answering these questions I rely in part on an eyewitness account by the revolutionary officer who was directly involved in the incident that led to the bloodbath. Henry Bowyer, Col. Abraham Buford's adjutant, rode forward with a flag of truce — after the action commenced — to advise Tarleton that Buford was now prepared to surrender.[46] According to Bowyer, "When close to the British commander, he delivered Beaufort's [sic] message, but a ball at the moment striking the forehead of Tarleton's horse, he plunged and both fell to the ground, the horse being uppermost."[47] Exasperated at the dishonouring of the flag, and fearing that Tarleton was dead, his cavalry reacted, in Tarleton's own words, with "a vindictive severity not easily restrained."[48] He — pinioned beneath his horse — was, as he implies, in no position easily to restrain them. Upwards of one hundred of Buford's corps were killed, many mangled, whereas Tarleton's casualties came to only nineteen.

Whilst running amok cannot be remotely condoned, no matter what the justification for it, it remains debatable whether the effect on the revolutionary mind was as marked as we have long been led to believe. If the action had not occurred, I conclude that the revolutionaries of the Carolinas, embittered against their neighbours and unfettered by civilised restraints, would most likely have continued to behave as badly as they did. "Tarleton's quarter," meaning no quarter, seems to have served simply as

---

311; McCrady, *History*, 519, 522; Robert D. Bass, *The Green Dragoon: The Lives of Banastre Tarleton and Mary Robinson* (reprint of 1958 edition, Columbia: Sandlapper Press Inc, 1973), 80-3; Russell F. Weigley, *The Partisan War: The South Carolina Campaign of 1780-1782* (Columbia: University of South Carolina Press, 1970), 7; Charles Bracelen Flood, *Rise and Fight Again: Perilous Times along the Road to Independence* (New York: Dodd, Mead and Co, 1976), 259-61; Lumkin, *From Savannah to Yorktown*, 50; J. Tracy Power, "'The Virtue of Humanity Was Totally Forgot': Buford's Massacre, May 29, 1780," *South Carolina Historical Magazine*, 93, No. 1 (January, 1992), 5-14; Buchanan, *The Road to Guilford Courthous*, 84-5; Wilson, *The Southern Strategy*, 259.
[46] For a biographical note on Buford, see CP, 1: 52.
[47] Alexander Garden Jr, *Anecdotes of the American Revolution (Second Series)* (Charleston, 1828), 126-8.
[48] Tarleton, *Campaigns*, 31.

an excuse. "After a review of the papers in volume I and subsequent volumes [of *The Cornwallis Papers*]," says Borick, "it is hard to disagree."[49]

The royal militia

The problem of finding suitable field officers and the fragility of the royal militia in South Carolina during the summer of 1780 I highlight in *The Cornwallis Papers*, basing myself on evidence coming to light there. Ill armed and at times slow to turn out, it displayed a patchwork of confidence, timidity, fidelity, and disloyalty in the face of the revolutionary forces taking to the field. Precipitated by Major Archibald McArthur's withdrawal from Cheraw Hill, Col. William Henry Mills' entire Pee Dee Regiment promptly defected, whilst in the backcountry most of Col. William Vernon Turner's Rocky Mount and Col. Matthew Floyd's Enoree-Tyger Regiments did likewise. Perhaps Col. John Fisher's Orangeburg Regiment was the most zealous, but other regiments in the backcountry were for the most part hesitant and in need of support, particularly those toward the North Carolina line. Overall, the fighting qualities of the royal militia were inevitably diminished, first by admitting disaffected persons, and second by incorporating Quiet men, as Ferguson termed them, to the extent of no more than one for every three loyalists.[50]

Whether we begin with Tarleton or continue with works down to the present day, we find that, while various authors relate the defection of Mills' and Floyd's regiments, none provides as complete a picture of the royal militia at this time as I do.[51]

---

[49] Carl P. Borick, Review, *The South Carolina Historical Magazine*, 112, Nos 1-2 (January-April, 2011), 89.
[50] For biographical notes on Fisher, McArthur, Mills, Floyd and Turner, see CP, 1: 80, 87, 132, 142 and 195. By "Quiet men" Ferguson meant those who had voiced neither loyalist nor revolutionary sentiments.
[51] See, for example, Tarleton, *Campaigns*, 93, 98.

What if the Battle of Camden had been lost?

Cornwallis's victory was so comprehensive that historians have been seemingly distracted into believing that it was inevitable. None — at least of those that I have read — has questioned Cornwallis's assertion that there was "little to lose by a defeat."[52] I on the contrary maintain that there was everything to lose — the war, in fact, itself. Why? Well, an army had been lost at Saratoga. If another had been lost at Camden, the political repercussions in Britain would have been so pronounced that, as with Yorktown, they would almost certainly have led to a termination of the war and a recognition of American independence.

No victory is inevitable. However propitious the prospects of success, chance invariably plays its part in battles and can be the determining factor.

Wemyss' and Moncrief's expeditions to the east of the Wateree and Santee

The day before Cornwallis quit Camden for North Carolina on 7 September 1780, Wemyss embarked on his expedition to the Pee Dee, designed to pacify the vast expanse of territory east of the Wateree no longer under British control. He had been ordered by Cornwallis to endeavour to form a militia in the Cheraw District, to disarm the untrustworthy, to make prisoners of those who had at first submitted — or lived quietly at home — and then revolted, to destroy or confiscate their property, and to hang those who had voluntarily enrolled in the royal militia and then gone over traitorously to the enemy. Wemyss set out from the High Hills of Santee with 80 to 100 men of the 63rd Regiment and was joined at Kingstree Bridge by detachments of the Royal North Carolina Regiment (100), Major John Harrison's irregular corps (50), and Col. Samuel Bryan's militia (50).[53] All were mounted. He burnt and laid waste about fifty houses and

---

[52] CP, 2: 12.
[53] For biographical notes on Harrison and Bryan, see CP, 1: 161 and 168.

plantations mostly belonging to those who had taken up arms in breach of their paroles or oaths of allegiance, but only some twenty prisoners were taken and only one man, "a notorious villain," having been convicted by court martial, was executed. Nothing could be done with forming a militia, the disaffection was so rife. Wemyss and his party arrived back at Camden on 4 October.[54]

As Wemyss prepared to march, Major James Moncrief with the 7th Regiment (Royal Fusiliers) quit Charlestown on 4 September to be joined two days later by Col. Elias Ball Sr's and Col. John Wigfall's militia at Lenud's Ferry. He proceeded to repossess Georgetown, where he assembled Col. James Cassells' militia, and went on to scour the lower parts of the district east of the Santee, destroying the property of those who had revolted, dispatching their slaves for the works at Charlestown, and appropriating some 150 horses for use to the north. After posting Ball and Wigfall at three ferries on Black River and leaving Cassells to patrol between there and the Pee Dee, he marched on the 21st for Camden, where he arrived one week later with the 7th (all mounted). The militia that he left behind performed as badly as usual. Shortly before midnight on the 28th Ball was routed by Col. Francis Marion at Black Mingo, Wigfall appears to have fled, and Cassells, fearing attack, evacuated Georgetown on the 29th or 30th, despite being protected by an offshore galley. The town was reoccupied three weeks later by a detachment sent from Charlestown.[55]

Although Wemyss and Moncrief did not overstep the rules of warfare of their day, writers down the years have criticised them for severity, turning a blind eye to that practised by revolutionary irregulars east of the Wateree and Santee ever since McArthur quit Cheraw Hill in mid July. Yes, they were

---

[54] CP, 2: 208-10, 214-7, and 219.
[55] Ibid., 266 and *passim*. For biographical notes on Ball, Moncrief, Cassells, Wigfall and Marion, see CP, 1: 51, 58, and 307; 2: 64; and 3: 4-5.

severe, but were their actions proportionate and defensible? That is the question. Cornwallis answered it in part when writing to Rawdon on 4 August: "It is absolutely necessary to inflict some exemplary punishment on the militia and inhabitants of that part of the country. On the moment we advance, we shall find an enemy in our rear ... some force must be sent to reduce and intimidate that country or the communication between the upper army and Charlestown will be impracticable."[56] In sanctioning the measures to be taken by Wemyss and Moncrief, Cornwallis came the closest he ever did to adopting in South Carolina the policy of deterrence favoured by Tarleton. The measures were in fact the only option available to him east of the Wateree and Santee, where the vast majority of the inhabitants were so virulently disaffected that lenity and conciliation stood no chance. They had to be tried, and indeed the devastation wrought by Wemyss and Moncrief may have prevented or deterred quite a few there from presenting a threat in the shorter term, but in the longer term the territory would remain a running sore while ever the British remained outside Charlestown. In other respects the expeditions failed. So short was Cornwallis of regular or British American troops to garrison the territory (those who took part in the expeditions being intended to reinforce him at Charlotte) that reliance had to be placed on militia to take their place. Yet, as I have mentioned, none could be formed by Wemyss, whilst those left by Moncrief were not up to the job. It has been argued — unconvincingly, it may be said — that the expeditions served only to turn many against the Crown, but the inhabitants there were already so preponderantly and actively opposed that this proposition is unfounded.

These, then, are the facts set out in, and the conclusions to be drawn from, *The Cornwallis Papers* — ones that contradict the material distortion of the historical record percolating down to the present day, as evinced by the accusation that Wemyss conducted a wholesale hanging spree. About Moncrief's foray

---

[56] CP, 1: 226.

history has remained virtually silent. Swisher summarises it very inaccurately in one brief sentence, but elsewhere we search almost in vain for references to it. [57]

Yorktown

If we begin with Major George Hanger, who took part in Clinton's failed attempt to relieve Cornwallis, and then turn to historians of the nineteenth and twentieth centuries whose interpretations have carried great weight, we find a uniformity of view that the single or prime cause of the capitulation was the Royal Navy's losing command of North American waters.

Discounting the defeats at King's Mountain and Cowpens as "only partial misfortunes," Hanger continues, "I will be so bold as to assert that these misfortunes did not in any degree contribute to the loss of America, nor could many such misfortunes have produced that calamity. Our ruin was completed by permitting *a superior French fleet* to ride triumphant on the American seas the autumn of 1781. That, and that only, ruined our cause in America and disgracefully put an end to the war. There the nail was clinched!"[58]

Among those agreeing with Hanger are Johnston, Carrington, and more recently Mackesy, Wallace and Ward. Others such as Adams and Robson concede that lost superiority at sea was the prime cause of the disaster but do not elaborate as to the rest. Willcox and Higginbotham are among those who mention that British military strategy was also at fault, but again without elaboration.[59]

---

[57] James K. Swisher, *The Revolutionary War in the Southern Back Country* (Gretna, LA: Pelican Publishing Co, 2012), 200.

[58] The Hon. George Hanger, *An Address to the Army in reply to Strictures of Roderick M'Kenzie (late Lieutenant in the 71st Regiment) on Tarleton's History of the Campaigns of 1780 and 1781* (London, 1789), 127-8.

[59] Henry P. Johnston, *The Yorktown Campaign and the Surrender of Cornwallis 1781* (reprint of 1881 edition, Williamstown, MA: Corner House Publishers, 1975), 97; Henry B. Carrington, *Battles of the American Revolution, 1775-1781*, (5th edition, New York, 1888), 654; Piers Mackesy, "British Strategy in the War of

While accepting that French naval superiority was the immediate cause of the defeat, I myself aver — unlike the historians I cite — that it was due preponderantly to a series of chance circumstances, a number of which, if they had been otherwise, would not have placed Cornwallis at Yorktown or would have averted his capitulation in other ways. So what were they? First, from any sensible strategic standpoint Cornwallis ought never to have been in Virginia in the first place.[60] Second, once he was there, and despite his marked reservations, he was pressured by Clinton to occupy the town.[61] The danger to such a post, if command of the Chesapeake was lost, it did not take an accomplished strategist to see[62] — and Clinton was aware that de Grasse was expected in the hurricane season.[63] Third, there was the coincidence of Yorktown's occupation with the arrival of de Grasse; fourth, was the failure of the Royal Navy to cater adequately for command of North American waters; fifth, was Cornwallis's decision not to break out at once; and ultimately, fate intervened, which in the form of a squall dispersed his boats and put paid to his breaking out on the Gloucester side at the close of the siege.

American Independence," *Yale Review*, 52 (Summer, 1963), 556-7; idem, *Could the British have won the War of Independence?* (Worcester, MA: Clark University Press, 1976), 25; Willard M. Wallace, *Appeal to Arms: A Military History of the American Revolution* (New York: Harper & Bros, 1951), 254; Christopher Ward, *The War of the Revolution* (New York: The Macmillan Co, 1952), 2: 885; Randolph G. Adams, "A View of Cornwallis's Surrender at Yorktown," *The American Historical Review*, 37, No. 1 (October, 1931), 49; Eric Robson, *The American Revolution in its Political and Military Aspects 1763-1783* (reprint of 1955 edition, New York: W W Norton & Co Inc, 1966), 146; William B. Willcox, "The British Road to Yorktown: A Study in Divided Command," *The American Historical Review*, 52, No. 1 (October, 1946), 26-7, 34; idem, "British Contributions to American Independence," *The Key Reporter*, 42, No. 1 (Autumn, 1976); Don Higginbotham, *The War of American Independence: Military Attitudes, Policies, and Practice, 1763-1789* (New York: The Macmillan Co, 1971), 383.

[60] See my first essay.

[61] See Clinton to Cornwallis, 8 and 11 July 1781, CP, 5: 140-3; and Cornwallis to Clinton, 26 July 1781, CP, 6: 13-15.

[62] See, for example, Clinton to Cornwallis, 29 May and 1 June 1781, CP, 5: 120.

[63] See Clinton to Cornwallis, 19 June 1781, ibid., 135.

As to the dilatoriness of the Royal Navy in repairing its fleet, I state in *The Cornwallis Papers*, without mentioning my source: "There is reason to suspect that the repairs to the ships damaged in the Battle of the Chesapeake Capes may not have been progressed as rapidly and as urgently as the critical situation demanded. Had they been completed one week sooner, Cornwallis might well have been saved."[64] In coming to these conclusions I had in mind comments made in his diary by Major Frederick Mackenzie, one of Clinton's aides-de-camp. On 1 October 1781 he remarks, "It appears very doubtful that the Navy will after all attempt or undertake any thing towards the relief of Lord Cornwallis." The captains "appear more ready to censure the conduct of others than to refit their own ships. Several of the captains spend more of their time on shore than they do on board and appear as unconcerned about the matter as if they commanded guard ships at Portsmouth." On 16 October he continues, "If the Navy are not a little more active, they will not get a sight of the Capes of Virginia before the end of this month and then it will be too late. They do not seem to be hearty in the business or to think that the saving that army is an object of such material consequence."[65]

Cornwallis has at times been criticised for abandoning his outer line of defence, for not breaking out immediately on the arrival of the French fleet, or for leaving too late his attempt to do so.[66] Although such factors are undeniably part of the chain that contributed to his defeat, I refute such charges in *The Cornwallis Papers* and explain why in my opinion his conduct was unexceptionable — in fact perfectly understandable in the circumstances.[67]

---

[64] CP, 6: 5.

[65] Allen French ed., *Diary of Frederick Mackenzie* (Cambridge, MA: Harvard University Press, 1930), 2: 653, 664. For a biographical note on Mackenzie, see CP, 3: 38.

[66] See, for example, Johnston, *Yorktown Campaign*, 120-1; Willcox, 'The British Road to Yorktown," 26-7; Robson, *American Revolution*, 141; Higginbotham, *The War*, 381; and William Seymour, *The Price of Folly: British Blunders in the War of American Independence* (London: Brassey's (UK) Ltd, 1995), 227-8.

[67] CP, 6: 5-6.

Admittedly, after the French naval troops had joined up with Lafayette's men on 1 September, Cornwallis could have attacked them before the arrival of Washington's and Rochambeau's reinforcement and hopefully broken out, whether to retire to the Carolinas or to proceed to the north. Alternatively he could have broken out on the Gloucester side and attempted by rapid marches to reach New York. Yet either option would have involved the abandonment of numerous sick, artillery, stores and shipping, and under these circumstances it was entirely reasonable that he should have preferred to await news from Clinton of his intentions. In mid September Clinton's dispatches arrived, in which he undertook to embark with a reinforcement as soon as possible, and with this assurance Cornwallis, again quite reasonably, forsook for the time being all thoughts of breaking out.

Cornwallis has, as I say, been criticised for abandoning his outer line of defence, about half a mile beyond the inner, on the night of 29 September as the enemy began to invest Yorktown. Could it have been held, if only for a few days, defence of the post would have been protracted. Yet, observing that the enemy were taking measures that could not fail to turn his left flank in a short time, and having just received word from Clinton that there was every reason to expect his departure on 5 October, Cornwallis did not hesitate to withdraw within his inner works, conscious that he could hold out until Clinton's anticipated arrival. It is idle to try and second-guess his judgement now.

In his *Campaigns* Tarleton makes out a seemingly convincing case for breaking out on the Gloucester side soon after Major Charles Cochrane arrived on 10 October with Clinton's dispatch of the 30th.[68] In it Clinton indicated that his departure had fallen back at the earliest to the 12th but that even that date was subject to disappointment. Yes, the chances of a break-out would have

---

[68] Tarleton, *Campaigns*, 379-85. For a biographical note on Cochrane, see CP, 6: 39.

markedly improved if Cornwallis had acted promptly as Tarleton suggests, but in the circumstances in which he found himself it is perfectly understandable that, for the same reason as he had not abandoned his post earlier, Cornwallis should have decided to wait for relief until matters became critical. By the 16th they had become so and on that night he attempted to transfer his fit troops to the Gloucester side, but, as previously mentioned, fate in the form of a squall intervened, his boats were dispersed, and the attempt came to nought. He was then left with no option but to capitulate.

It remains for me here to add briefly to my comments about Washington. "Like all great commanders," says Robson, "he was aided by sheer good fortune."[69] I go one step further and suggest that, for the reasons I have advanced, he was a general who was not just lucky in the Yorktown campaign but extraordinarily so.

---

[69] Robson, *American Revolution*, 172.

∞ 3 ∞

Cornwallis and the autumn campaign of 1780 — His advance from Camden to Charlotte[1]

Throwing caution to the winds, Cornwallis embarked on the autumn campaign after his victory on 16 August 1780 at the Battle of Camden. Throughout the campaign a pressing concern would be the sickliness of the troops, whether they were those who marched with him or those who were intended to join him later from Camden.

An immediate problem, which delayed the march, was the formation of supply trains. Waggons there were aplenty, what with those taken in recent engagements and others pressed from Orangeburg and Ninety Six, but sadly horses, gear, conductors and drivers were wanting.

Another cause of delay was the severe lack of provision at Camden, exacerbated by additional mouths to feed after the recent battle. On 31 August Cornwallis remarked to Lt. Col. Nisbet Balfour, "Hitherto, so far from being able to get a few days' [*provision*] beforehand, which is absolutely necessary for our march, we are this day without either flour or meal and Tarleton's horses have had no forage since the action."[2]

---

[1] Cornwallis's dispatches to Germain and Clinton have for the most part been long in the public domain and have been relied on by historians to provide a broad outline of Cornwallis's advance to Charlotte. As in this essay, those accounts may now be supplemented with much more detailed information based on my edition of *The Cornwallis Papers: The Campaigns of 1780 and 1781 in the Southern Theatre of the American Revolutionary War*, 6 vols (Uckfield: The Naval & Military Press Ltd, 2010) ("CP").

[2] CP: 2, 66.

Against all the odds Cornwallis managed to assemble a proviant train of thirty-eight waggons by 7 September, twenty of which were loaded with a puncheon of rum in each and the rest with flour and salt. At daybreak, accompanied by two 3-pounders, he marched towards Charlotte with the 23rd Regiment (Royal Welch Fusiliers), 33rd Regiment and Volunteers of Ireland, leaving behind material numbers of their dead, sick and wounded. Two days later he reached the border settlement at the Waxhaws and was joined by Col. Samuel Bryan's North Carolina militia. The troops soon set up camp on Waxhaw Creek, living on wheat collected and ground from the plantations in the neighbourhood, most of which were owned by Scotch-Irish revolutionaries who had fled.

On 8 September Lt. Col. Banastre Tarleton crossed the Wateree at Camden Ferry and advanced with the British Legion and a detachment of the 71st Regiment's light troops towards White's Mill on Fishing Creek. While there on the 17th, he fell ill of a violent attack of yellow fever. His entire command was now needed to protect him and it was not until the 23rd that he became well enough to be moved to Blair's Mill on the eastern side of the Catawba. Crossing on the same day at the ford there, which was six hundred yards wide and three and a half feet deep, the Legion joined Cornwallis. All in all, Tarleton's illness was one of the main reasons for setting back the entry into Charlotte. It took place on the 26th.

By then Cornwallis had been reinforced by the 71st, but both battalions were much depleted, not only by their dead and wounded in the Battle of Camden, but also by their sick who had fallen down earlier at Cheraw Hill. Many, who were recovering, had relapsed before their march and returned to the hospital at Camden. Accompanied by a detachment of artillery with two 6-pounders, a few pioneers, the convalescents of the 33rd, and two supply trains, one of rum and salt, and the other of artillery stores, arms and ammunition, the remains of the 71st arrived at the Waxhaws on the 21st, but they too were in poor shape,

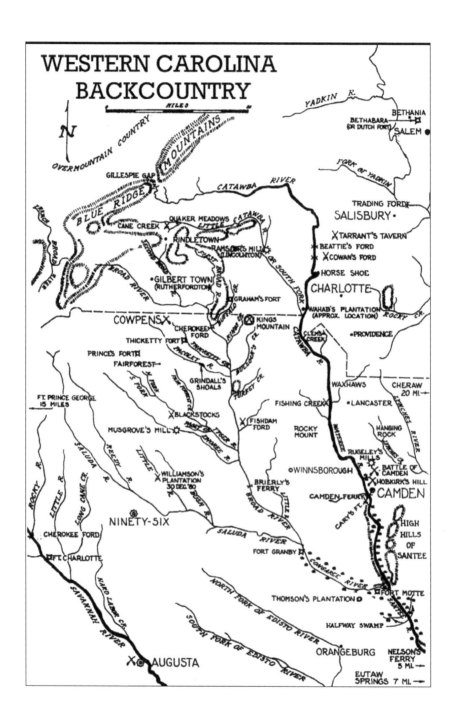

WESTERN CAROLINA BACKCOUNTRY

MILES

N

OVERMOUNTAIN COUNTRY

BLUE RIDGE MOUNTAINS

YADKIN R.

BETHANIA
BETHABARA
(OR DUTCH FORT)
SALEM

FORK OR YADKIN

GILLESPIE GAP

CATAWBA RIVER

TRADING FORD
SALISBURY•

FRENCH BROAD RIVER

CANE CREEK
QUAKER MEADOWS
LITTLE CATAWBA
RINDLETOWN
RAMSOUR'S MILLS
(LINCOLNTON)

LITTLE OR SOUTH FORK

XTARRANT'S TAVERN
XBEATTIE'S FORD
XCOWAN'S FORD

HORSE SHOE
CHARLOTTE

BROAD RIVER

GILBERT TOWN
(RUTHERFORDTON)
GRAHAM'S FORT

FLINT BROAD R.

BUFFALO

KINGS CR.

KINGS MOUNTAIN

WAHAB'S PLANTATION
(APPROX. LOCATION)

ROCKY CR.

COWPENSX
CHEROKEE FORD
THICKETTY FORT
PRINCE'S FORT
FAIRFOREST→

THICKETTY CR.

PACOLET R.

BULLOCK'S CR.

CLEMS CREEK

CATAWBA R.

•PROVIDENCE

N. FORK
S. FORK

PAIR FORREST R.

GRINDALL'S SHOALS

TURKEY CR.

WAXHAWS

CHERAW
20 MI.→

FT. PRINCE GEORGE
15 MILES

XBLACKSTOCKS

HANS OR TYGER R.

FISHING CREEKX

•LANCASTER

LYNCHES RIVER

MUSGROVE'S MILL☼

FISHDAM FORD

ROCKY MOUNT

WATEREE

HANGING ROCK

SALUDA R.

RELLY R.

LITTLE R.

WILLIAMSON'S PLANTATION
30 DEC. '80

TYGER R.

BRIERLY'S FERRY

BROAD RIVER

LITTLE R.

RUGELEY'S MILLS
BATTLE OF CAMDEN
HOBKIRK'S HILL
CAMDEN

ROCKY R.

LITTLE R.

LONG CANE CR.

NINETY-SIX

CHEROKEE FORD

☼FT. CHARLOTTE

SALUDA RIVER

CAMDEN FERRY
CART'S FT.

HIGH HILLS OF SANTEE

HARD LABOR CR.

SAVANNAH RIVER

FORT GRANBY

CONGAREE RIVER

NORTH FORK OF EDISTO RIVER
SOUTH FORK OF EDISTO RIVER

THOMSON'S PLANTATION ◉

HALFWAY SWAMP

FORT MOTTE

X☼ AUGUSTA

ORANGEBURG

NELSON'S FERRY
5 MI.→

EUTAW SPRINGS 7 MI.→

adding considerably to the sick of the other regiments there, who by that date amounted to above 120 and were daily increasing. When Cornwallis advanced to Charlotte, the debris of the 71st was left at Waxhaw Creek to form a staging post.

Meanwhile Lt. Col. James Wemyss[3] and Major James Moncrief had been engaged on their two expeditions designed to pacify the vast expanse of territory east of the Wateree and Santee that was no longer under British control. They failed miserably and both had returned to Camden by early October.[4]

Like Wemyss and Moncrief, Major Patrick Ferguson, the Inspector of Militia, had been busy too. In compliance with Cornwallis's instructions he left Sugar Creek for Camden on 23 August to discuss the part to be played by his corps and the backcountry militia in forthcoming operations. He rejoined his corps on 1 September near Fair Forest Creek, having obtained Cornwallis's approval to his making a rather hazardous advance into Tryon County, North Carolina, the purpose of which was to secure the left of Cornwallis's march. He was then to join the troops at Charlotte so that his corps and the militia might accompany the onward advance. Having crossed the frontier on the 7th, he proceeded to pass some time in and around Gilbert Town, defeating Col. Charles McDowell at Cane Creek on the 12th. He then attempted to settle the county by disarming the disaffected and putting their arms into the hands of loyalists who came in. On the 14th he had some 650 militia with him, but they were old and infirm and part neither armed nor trained. By the 28th, when he was seeking to intercept Lt. Col. Elijah Clark, his militia had increased to under 800, but of what quality he does not say. In the meantime he had mustered 500 loyalists within twenty-five miles of Gilbert Town, "half of whom are of the first class and arm'd," while another body nearly as numerous

---

[3] Pronounced "Weems".
[4] For an account of the expeditions and a justification for them, see my second essay.

had been formed on the Catawba from its head forty miles downwards. Aware by now of the revolutionary parties gathering to oppose him, he was confident that, centrical as he was, he would prevent a general junction and remain master of the field. He could have not been more egregiously mistaken.

As Cornwallis lingered at the Waxhaws, Clark, who had returned with about 200 men to the Ceded Lands in Georgia, incited some 500 more to join him and on 14 September made a surprise attack on Lt. Col. Thomas Brown's post at Augusta. It was a close-run thing. Brown held out courageously but was saved only by the spirited and active conduct of Lt. Col. John Harris Cruger, who came promptly from Ninety Six to his relief. Clark with many of his party fled across the Savannah River and crossed some two weeks later into North Carolina, going off at the head of Saluda at a gap beyond Ferguson's reach. After the attack severe measures were taken to pacify the Ceded Lands.[5]

Of the 2nd division intended to reinforce Cornwallis at Charlotte, only the 7th Regiment (Royal Fusiliers) came up, much depleted by 106 sick left behind at Camden. Accompanying it were 150 convalescents — some for the 23rd, some for the 33rd, and the rest for the 71st — and a supply train of ten puncheons of rum and fifty-six bushels of salt. On 5 October they all arrived at the Waxhaws, and two days later the 7th, but not the convalescents, advanced to Charlotte. The rest of the 2nd division consisting of the Wemyss' 63rd Regiment and Lt Colonel John Hamilton's Royal North Carolina Regiment never came up. Of the 71st, which had been posted at the Waxhaws, the 2nd Battalion was ordered forward on the 1 October, whereas the 1st Battalion, which had initially been intended to meet Ferguson at Armour's Ford,[6] was given its marching orders on the 8th.

---

[5] "The Ceded Lands" was an expression commonly used to refer to part of the territory ceded to Georgia by the Cherokees and Creeks in 1773. It was located in the up country above Augusta, extending from the headwaters of the Oconee downwards and between that river and the Savannah.
[6] The ford lay near the mouth of the south fork of the Catawba. It was deep and crossing was at times dangerous.

Together, they would have brought to Charlotte the numerous sick and convalescents left behind with them.

On 7 October Cornwallis explained his plan of campaign to Wemyss:

> The object of marching into North Carolina is only to raise men, which, from every account I have received of the number of our friends, there is great reason to hope may be done to a very considerable amount. For this purpose I shall move in about ten or twelve days to Salisbury and from thence invite all loyalists of the neighbouring countys to repair to our standard to be formed into Provincial corps and armed, clothed and appointed as soon as we can do it. From thence I mean to move my whole force down to Cross Creek *[to raise the Highlanders]*. As it will then be about the middle of November, I hope the lower country will be healthy. I shall then be in full communication with our shipping and shall receive all the arms and clothing that Charlestown can afford.[7]

Wemyss, who had been intended to command an intermediate post at Charlotte, now to be abandoned due to the inveteracy of the locality, was instructed to operate again east of Camden before joining Cornwallis at Cross Creek, but his orders were almost immediately countermanded.

For Cornwallis, overstretched as he was, it was now that the chickens came home to roost.

Of the risks he was running, some would have been apparent to him at the start of the campaign, aware as he was that it might be an imprudent measure. Among the greatest risks was that of losing control of much of South Carolina and Georgia, so few were the troops that he left behind. Charlestown and Savannah were safe, but what about the rest of the country? If we leave aside the relative backwater of Georgetown, there were only three

---

[7] CP: 2, 222.

principal posts in South Carolina and Georgia outside Charlestown and Savannah — at Camden, the village of Ninety Six, and Augusta. Left to garrison Camden were the New York Volunteers and the South Carolina Royalist Regiment under the overall command of Lt. Col. George Turnbull. According to him, the South Carolina Royalists, who did not arrive until 17 September, made a very sorry appearance and on the 22nd did duty for no more than 160 rank and file. By 2 October only 91 of them were fit for duty, as some had fallen down with the small pox and others presumably with the other illnesses prevalent there. Two days later those fit for duty in both corps came to a total of 247. Admittedly, part of the Royal North Carolina Regiment was also at Camden in September, as was the debris of the 63rd, and both were augmented by the arrival of Wemyss' party at the beginning of October. Yet neither corps formed part of the garrison, for both were awaiting orders (which never came) to reinforce Cornwallis. On 20 October the three British American regiments afforded no more than 300 men fit for duty. All in all, given the need to maintain the post of Camden itself, the garrison had precious few troops for exerting control over the vast expanse of territory dependent on it or for supporting the royal militia to this end. Alone, the royal militia were in Turnbull's eyes a busted flush. As he would soon observe, "... our officers of militia in general are not near so active as the rebels, and great numbers of their privates are ready to turn against us when an opportunity offers ... Depend on it, militia will never do any good without regular troops."[8] With so few troops in the garrison to support them, the militia were, if attacked, an edifice waiting to crumble, far beyond the reach of Cornwallis to sustain them if he had penetrated deeper into North Carolina, taking Ferguson, the 63rd and the Royal North Carolina Regiment with him. That was the risk. Nor would it have been markedly lessened if an intermediate post under Wemyss had been established

---

[8] CP: 2, 250.

at Charlotte, so composed would it have been of convalescents. The risk was in fact low for only so long as Cornwallis remained within reach, Wemyss and Hamilton were not brought up to reinforce him, and Ferguson continued to protect the northern border against incursions. Even so, control of the area east of Camden had long been lost, and despite Wemyss' and Moncrief's expeditions, nothing could be done to reassert it. Cornwallis desperately sought to scrape the barrel at Camden for a further foray there, but all to no avail. Nothing really effective could be done but to advance Col. Samuel Tynes' militia to the forks of Black River, where they were promptly routed by Lt. Col. Francis Marion, and to await Tarleton's punitive but brief incursion in November.

The situation at Ninety Six was pretty parlous too. Garrisoning the village were the 1st Battalion, De Lancey's Brigade, and the 3rd Battalion, New Jersey Volunteers, under the overall command of Cruger. He had with him near 300 men fit for duty. As with Camden, the problem was not so much the post itself as the extensive hinterland. Split as it was into tracts of loyalists and revolutionaries, the most worrying parts were the Long Canes settlement and the tract contiguous to it, being the catchment areas of Col. Richard King's and Lt. Col. Moses Kirkland's regiments. There the inhabitants were preponderantly disaffected and the bulk of the two regiments was not to be relied on. Of almost equal concern was a rebellious tract of fifty miles about the Tyger and Enoree, where the inhabitants had mostly fled and were waiting for Cornwallis and Ferguson to move on before they returned and commenced hostilities. In general the royal militia left behind by Ferguson were reluctant to turn out, and in any event Cruger was exceedingly short of men to support them. With Ferguson on the northern border and on his march to join Cornwallis, Cruger was of opinion that, if a tenuous hold on the district was to be maintained, a body of regular or British American troops was essential to occupy the area between the Broad and Saluda Rivers vacated by Ferguson. Unfortunately, none was available, and so there was a high risk that the district would be overrun. An intermediate post, if established at Charlotte, would have been too remote to have any effect.

Despite the defeat of Clark, the British hold on the back parts of Georgia remained tenuous. We have no record of the casualties sustained at Augusta, but at the time of Clark's attack Brown's garrison consisted of 199 men of the King's Rangers fit for duty, 35 members of the Indian Department, 100 convalescents of the King's Rangers and New Jersey Volunteers, and 500 native Americans who happened to be visiting the village. After the attack Cruger left upwards of 200 militia to complete the work of scouring the Ceded Lands. With so remarkably few troops and militia to maintain control of Augusta and the hinterland, the door remained open to enemy incursions.

Overall, the situation was ripe for disaster.

∞ 4 ∞

How many troops did Cornwallis actually bring to the Battle of Guilford?

Works about the American Revolutionary War are littered with references to troop numbers, whether to rank and file or not, and betray some confusion between the two. On analysing British and British American regimental returns I discovered that the proportion of officers, staff, non-commissioned officers and drummers was consistently 17.5% of all ranks. I apply this factor to rank and file returns in order to calculate Tarleton's total force at the Battle of Cowpens,[1] Cornwallis's remaining force for the

---

[1] If we take Tarleton's total force at Cowpens, I accurately calculate it as 1,150 men (Ian Saberton ed., *The Cornwallis Papers: The Campaigns of 1780 and 1781 in the Southern Theatre of the American Revolutionary War* (Uckfield: The Naval & Military Press Ltd, 2010) ("CP"), 3: 11). Whereas the likes of Higginbotham, Waring and Ward agree with me, others such as Hunter, Schenck and Treacy put the figure as low as 850. By contrast Bass, Carrington, Fortescue, Graham and the Wickwires are among those who specify a figure of 1,000 (Christopher Ward, *The War of the Revolution* (New York: The Macmillan Co., 1952), 2: 755; M. F. Treacy, *Prelude to Yorktown: The Southern Campaigns of Nathanael Greene 1780-81* (Chapel Hill: University of North Carolina Press), 111; Robert D. Bass, *The Green Dragoon: The Lives of Banastre Tarleton and Mary Robinson* (reprint of 1958 edition, Columbia SC: Sandlapper Press Inc, 1973), 143, 147, 159; Sir John Fortescue, *A History of the British Army* (London: Macmillan & Co., 1902), 3: 359; Franklin and Mary Wickwire, *Cornwallis: The American Adventure* (Boston MA: Houghton Mifflin Co., 1970), 256; Alice N. Waring, *The Fighting Elder: Andrew Pickens (1739-1817)* (Columbia: University of South Carolina Press, 1962), 47; Henry B. Carrington, *Battles of the American Revolution, 1775-1781* (5th edition, New York, 1888), 542; Don Higginbotham, *Daniel Morgan: Revolutionary Rifleman* (Chapel Hill: University of North Carolina Press, 1961), 130; Cyrus Lee Hunter, *Sketches of Western North Carolina ... illustrating principally the Revolutionary Period* (Raleigh NC, 1877), 333; David Schenck, *North Carolina 1780-81* (Raleigh NC, 1889), 219; James Graham, *The Life of General Daniel Morgan* (New York, 1856), 277-8).

winter campaign,[2] and use it in attempting to re-assess Cornwallis's total force at the Battle of Guilford — all of which had previously been uncertain. That the factor is accurate is borne out by the correlation of the two returns, one for rank and file appearing in *The Cornwallis Papers*, and the other for all ranks provided by Johnston, that capitulated at Yorktown.[3]

So how many troops did Cornwallis actually bring to the field at Guilford? If we take the return of rank and file fit for duty on 1 March 1781,[4] we find that due to attrition the figure (excluding artillery) had decreased from 2,440 to 2,213 in one month, a loss of 227 men. If we then allow proportionately for continuing attrition between then and March 15, the date of the battle, we arrive at a figure of 2,137, giving, when we extrapolate by the factor of 17.5%, the figure of 2,511 for all ranks. Yet before the battle Cornwallis had detached the Royal North Carolina Regiment (221 rank and file as proportionately reduced by attrition), 100 infantry and 20 cavalry with the waggons and baggage towards Bell's Mill on Deep River. If we increase the total by 17.5% to cover all ranks, we arrive at an overall figure of 341, leaving Cornwallis with a total of 2,170 men (excluding artillery) brought by him to the battle. On the other hand, according to

---

[2] Accurately calculated by me as some 2,850 men by extrapolating by a factor of 17.5% from a return for rank and file (CP, 3: 12 and 4: 61-2).

[3] According to Johnston, the besiegers numbered 5,500 Continentals, 7,500 French, and 3,000 militia — a total of 16,000, and he calculates the besieged to be 7,500, though they were in fact 225 fewer. Of those that capitulated, the return of 18 October 1781 appearing in the CP lists 5,950 rank and file, and when we extrapolate by using the factor of 17.5% to cater for officers etc., we arrive at a figure of 6,991 for all ranks. If from the return of 27 October provided by Johnston we subtract the staff of the public departments, followers of the army, pioneers, and odds and sods not listed in the former return, the figure is 6,949 for all ranks, so that the two returns correlate, as it is reasonable to assume that some of the severely wounded had died in the interval before the latter return was prepared. Not accounted for in the above figures are some 800 marines (CP, 6: 6 and 116-7; Henry P. Johnston, *The Yorktown Campaign and the Surrender of Cornwallis 1781* (reprint of 1881 edition, Williamstown MA: Corner House Publishers, 1975), 164-5).

[4] CP, 4: 61-2.

the return of troops who fought there, the number for all ranks was 1,924 (including 50 artillery), leaving, when we subtract the artillery, 296 men unaccounted for. Quite simply, the two returns do not correlate.[5]

Can we then resolve the impasse? I believe so. In his dispatch of 10 April, Cornwallis reports to Clinton that his force was 1,360 infantry, rank and file, and about 200 cavalry.[6] When writing to Phillips on 26 April[7] Clinton remarks that he was totally at a loss to conjecture how Cornwallis's numbers were so reduced, and indeed there are solid reasons for questioning whether an astute battlefield commander like Cornwallis would ever have been prepared to risk a general action in which his force was so depleted. While the figure for Tarleton's cavalry is accurate,[8] that given for Cornwallis's rank and file cannot fail to be suspect. So what can have led to it? Well, in the eighteenth century there was a marked similarity in the way in which "3" and "8" were written, so much so that, if "8" was written badly, it was at times easy to confuse the two. A copyist may well have made this mistake when preparing for signature Cornwallis's dispatch to Clinton. In that event the correct figure should have been 1,860 (presumably including artillery) which, when we extrapolate by using the factor of 17.5%, gives a combined figure of 2,185. When added to the figure of 200 for cavalry, Cornwallis's total force would have amounted to 2,385, not too far from the figure of 2,220 (2,170 plus 50 artillery) calculated by me above on the basis of the first return mentioned in my second paragraph.

Problem solved?

---

[5] CP, 4: 61-3.
[6] CP, 4: 109.
[7] CP, 5: 51.
[8] CP, 3: 11.

∞ 5 ∞

From Yorktown to England —
Cornwallis's fraught passage home

Based preponderantly on *The Cornwallis Papers*,[1] this essay describes in part Cornwallis's last days in Virginia, his brief sojourn in New York, and events thereafter leading up to his arrival in London.

Immediately after the capitulation of Yorktown and Gloucester Cornwallis began to write his letter of 20 October 1781 reporting the outcome of the siege to Clinton.[2] He wrote it, he says, "under great agitation of mind and in great hurry, being constantly interrupted by numbers of people coming upon business or ceremonies." In fact the interruptions were becoming so great that he had sought the assistance of the French in order to exercise some measure of control, as evinced by the following letter:

> A bord de *l'Experiment* en rade de York
> le 21 8bre 1781

Milord

Vous desirés une garde a bord de votre parlementaire pour empecher les Americains d'aller y troubler vos operations. Je viens, d'après votre demande transmise par Monsieur de Grandchain, d'ordonner une garde de 4 hommes et un caporal pour s'y transporter et prendre la consigne de l'officier qu'il y trouvera de votre part, et qui puise connoitre ceux qui

---

[1] Ian Saberton ed., *The Cornwallis Papers: The Campaigns of 1780 and 1781 in the Southern Theatre of the American Revolutionary War*, 6 vols (Uckfield: The Naval & Military Press Ltd, 2010) ("CP").
[2] CP: 6, 125-9.

doivent aborder or non. Veuilles bien leur faire donner un emplacement pour se coucher. J'ay fait pourvoir a leur nourriture.

J'ay l'honeur de vous le repeter, milord, je seray toujours empressé de saisir les occasions ou je pourray prouver qu'on ne peut ajouter au respect avec lequel j'ay l'honeur d'etre, milord,

Votre tres humble et tres obeissant serviteur

MARTELLI CHEVALIER

TRANSLATION

On board *l'Expériment* in York road
October 21, 1781

My Lord

You desire a guard on board your flag vessel to prevent the Americans from going and disturbing your operations there. In compliance with your request, transmitted by Monsieur de Grandchain,[3] I have just ordered a guard of four men and a corporal to be transported there and to take orders from the officer of yours that he will find there and who may know those who are to go on board or not. Please have a bunk provided for them to sleep in. I have taken care of their provisions.

I have the honour to repeat, My Lord, that I shall be most ready to seize every opportunity of proving to you that it is not possible to add to the respect with which I have the honour to be, My Lord,

Your very humble and very obedient servant

THE CHEVALIER MARTELLI[4]

---

[3] Grandchain was a French naval officer who had been one of three commissioners appointed by the enemy to finalise the articles of capitulation before the lines of York. He represented the French fleet, the Vicomte de Noailles the French army, and Lt. Col. John Laurens the American revolutionary forces. (Thomas Balch, *French in America during the War of Independence of the United States 1777-1783* (London: Ardent Media Ltd, 1972).

[4] CP: 6, 136-7. Apart from commanding the man of war *'l'Expériment,* with which he would take part in the engagement off Saints Passage between Guadeloupe and Dominica in April 1782, Martelli has not been identified.

69

Of pressing concern to Cornwallis was how to protect those loyalists particularly obnoxious to the enemy who had been serving or assisting him in either a military or civil capacity. If they remained prisoners, they were liable to be brought rigorously before revolutionary courts with the risk that, if found guilty, for example of treason, they might be sentenced to death. Cornwallis did lessen the problem to some degree by straining article 8 of the capitulation so as to extend from troops to civilians the persons who, without examination, might sail for New York with his dispatches in the *Bonetta* sloop of war. Yet more was needed, given that article 10, which would have provided comprehensive protection for loyalists, was not granted by the enemy. So Cornwallis came to a tacit agreement with Washington — who did not wish to sully his victory with the blood of his prisoners — whereby Cornwallis was permitted to spirit away in flag vessels, for example the *Andrew*, *Cochran* and *Lord Mulgrave*, those loyalists who feared falling foul of revolutionary law. Not a party to the agreement was Gov. Thomas Nelson Jr. of Virginia,[5] whose following two letters to Cornwallis illustrate the nature of the problem:

October 20th, 1781

Rt. Hon. Lt. General Earl Cornwallis

My Lord

I have been informed that a number of the refugees from this State and also negroes are attempting to make their escape by getting on board the *Bonetta* sloop of war. As they will endeavour to lie concealed from your Lordship's notice till the vessel sails, I have thought it necessary to make this communication to you that you may take measures to prevent the State and individuals from sustaining an injury of this nature.

I have the honour to be
Your Lordship's obedient and humble servant

THO[S] NELSON Jr

---

[5] For a biographical note on Nelson, see CP: 5, 110.

October 21st, 1781

The Rt. Hon. Lt. General Earl Cornwallis

My Lord

I have received your verbal message respecting two citizens of this State, the Reverend Mr William Andrews and the Reverend Mr Harrison, who joined the British army after its arrival here and who are now delivered up into the hands of the civil power. The laws of this country have fixed the mode of proceeding against persons guilty of such conduct and we are ignorant of any power which has a right to supersede their force. By these laws, enacted by their own representatives, they shall be fairly and impartially tried and they must abide their sentence.

I am informed that Lt. Colonel Simcoe has refused to deliver up a certain Christopher Robinson who now bears a commission in his corps but who deserted from the actual service of the State. The articles of capitulation cannot justify this detention and I shall by no means acquiesce in it. It is my wish to treat those men whom the fortune of war has put into our power with that civility which their situation claims and it would give me pain to be constrained in any instance to act in a different manner. Your Lordship in the case under consideration has, I imagine, the power of preventing it and I flatter myself you will at once see the propriety of exercising this power.

I have the honour to be
Your Lordship's obedient and very humble servant

THO^S NELSON Jr[6]

Of the two clergymen seized by Nelson, William Andrews was an Irishman who was rector of the Anglican church at Portsmouth. He had arrived in Virginia in 1773 after ministering for a few years in New York. A wavering loyalist, who at a 4 July celebration in 1780 had publicly denounced the Declaration of Independence as "improper and impolitick," he had been

---

[6] CP: 6, 134-6.

appointed chaplain to the garrison at Portsmouth in 1781. Having fallen captive at the capitulation of Yorktown, he would be allowed to go home before being indicted in March 1782 for high treason by the justices at Norfolk. He would not, however, stand trial, receiving a gubernatorial pardon for "the treason of which he was not convicted," and took passage for England. In October 1783, while at Chelsea, he presented to the royal commission a claim for compensation in respect of his confiscated property in Virginia, and two years later was residing in Glasgow.[7]

William Harrison was an Anglican clergyman in Dinwiddie County who had resigned his benefice several months before being appointed chaplain to the garrison at Gloucester. Ambivalent in his politics, he had previously served as chairman of his county's committee of safety. Having now fallen captive, like Andrews, at the capitulation, he too would be allowed to go home, but when he was brought before the examining court of Dinwiddie County on an indictment of high treason, he was acquitted, "no evidence appearing against him." He did not return to the ministry full-time but took up residence in Petersburg, where he was elected to the Common Council, to the Board of Aldermen, and finally to the office of Mayor.[8]

As to Christopher Robinson, he like so many other loyalists in his situation would escape Nelson's clutches and be spirited away from Virginia in one of the flag vessels. Commissioned an ensign in the infantry of Lt. Col. John Graves Simcoe's Queen's Rangers on 26 June 1781, he had been born into a family prominent in the public life of Virginia, attending the College of William

---

[7] Otto Lohrenz, "William Andrews," *Southern Studies*, xxiv (1985); idem, "The advantage of rank and status: Thomas Price, a Loyalist parson of Revolutionary Virginia," *The Historian*, lx (1998); Peter Wilson Coldham, *American Loyalist Claims* (Washington, DC: National Genealogical Society, 1980).

[8] Otto Lohrenz, "The Right Reverend William Harrison of Revolutionary Virginia, First 'Lord Archbishop of America'," *Historical Magazine of the Protestant Episcopal Church*, liii (1984); idem, *supra, The Historian*, lx (1998).

and Mary at Williamsburg. At the close of the war he would be placed on the British half-pay list and settle in New Brunswick before moving on to Quebec. In 1792 he took up residence in Kingston, when Simcoe, now Lt. Governor of Upper Canada, appointed him Surveyor General of Woods and Forests there. In 1794 he was licensed to practise law and two years later was returned to the House of Assembly as the member for Ontario and Addington, promoting in due course a bill, which was not enacted, "to enable persons migrating into this province to bring their negro slaves into the same." He died cut off from most of his family in Virginia, one of the few Robinsons there to be of the loyalist persuasion.[9]

Cornwallis did not deign to reply to Nelson's letters and the removal of affected loyalists from Yorktown proceeded as Cornwallis and Washington had tacitly agreed.

Little else of importance was left for Cornwallis to resolve. As far as his troops were concerned, they were marched off as prisoners to camps in Virginia and Maryland under the guard of militia. After being wined and dined by Washington, Rochambeau and other revolutionary and French officers, Cornwallis and his officers entered into paroles and were permitted to go to New York, Charlestown or Europe. One officer per fifty men remained behind to reside with the rest of the prisoners.

On his arrival at New York Cornwallis wrote to Rochambeau confirming that certain naval arrangements explicit or implicit in the capitulation would be met and thanked him for his kindness and courtesy:

---

[9] *Dictionary of Canadian Biography* (University of Toronto, 1982); WO 65/164(31) (Kew: UK National Archives).

Nouvelle York
Novembre 25 1781

Son Excellence le Comte de Rochambeau etc. etc. etc.

Monsieur

Après un trajet très désagreable je suis arrive ici le 19 de ce mois.

L'Amiral Digby a eu la bonté de promettre de faire partir le *Bonetta* sans perte de tems et d'envoyer à son bord tous les François qui sont à présent prisonniers ici. Un nombre suffisant de prisonniers americains seront envoyés pour naviguer et seront chargés de vous livrer les autres parlementaires le plutôt qu'il sera possible, et si ce nombre n'egale pas le nombre des notres qui arrivent dans ces parlementaires, l'Amiral se tiendra responsable de vous rendre compte du reste à votre satisfaction. Le parlementaire nommé le *Cochran* fera voile dans peu de jours; celui nommé l'*Andrew* n'arriva qu' hier mais, ayant fait eau dangereusement dans deux places, ne peut pas sortir avant d'être reparé; et nous n'avons pas encore reçu des nouvelles de celui nommé le *Lord Mulgrave*.

Capitaine Dundas se charge de quelque fromage et de porter anglois, que je vous prie de me faire l'honneur d'agréer.

C'est avec des sentiments de la plus vive reconnoissance qui ne seront jamais effacés que je presente à votre Excellence mes très humbles re-merciments pour toutes vos bontés et politesses. Il me fera le plaisir le plus sensible de saisir toutes les occasions qui pourront se presenter de montrer la consideration et l'estime la plus parfaite avec laquelle j'ai honneur d'être, monsieur, etc.

[CORNWALLIS]

TRANSLATION

New York
November 25, 1781

His Excellency le Comte de Rochambeau etc. etc. etc.

Sir

After a very tiresome passage I arrived here on the 19th instant.

Admiral Digby has kindly promised to dispatch the *Bonetta* without loss of time and to send on board her all the Frenchmen who are now prisoners here. A sufficiency of American prisoners shall be sent to navigate and be charged with delivering up to you the other flag vessels as soon as it can be done, and if these men are not equal in number to ours coming in these flag vessels, the Admiral will hold himself responsible for accounting for the rest to your satisfaction. The flag named the *Cochran* will set sail in a few days; the one named the *Andrew* arrived only yesterday, but having sprung a dangerous leak in two places, it cannot leave until it is repaired; and we have as yet no news of the one named the *Lord Mulgrave*.

Captain Dundas has taken charge of some English cheese and porter, which I beg you will do me the honour of accepting.[10]

With sentiments of the warmest gratitude which will never be effaced, may I express to Your Excellency my very humble acknowledgements for all your acts of kindness and courtesy. It will give me the most heartfelt pleasure to seize every opportunity that may offer for demonstrating the respect and most perfect esteem with which I have the honour to be, sir, etc.

[CORNWALLIS][11]

The period from Cornwallis's arrival in New York till his departure for England is chiefly notable for the beginning of the Clinton-Cornwallis controversy, a distasteful spectacle in which each sought to offload on to the other responsibility for the Yorktown disaster, whereas in reality both were in part to blame. Cornwallis for his part ought never to have marched into Virginia in the first place, while Clinton, once Cornwallis was there, brought undue pressure on him to return to Williamsburg Neck, tacitly acquiescing, despite Cornwallis's reservations, in the choice of Yorktown as the only place to protect ships of the line.

Clinton's letter of 2 and 10 December[12] is in particular misleading, where he asserts that his promises of relief, held out

---

[10] For biographical notes of Dundas and Digby, see CP: 3,55 and 5, 189.
[11] CP: 6,164-5.
[12] CP: 6, 158-161.

in his letters of 2 and 6 September,[13] might have been frustrated by the navy, though no such assertions were made at the time. It was reasonable for Cornwallis to assume, as he did, that Clinton was speaking in the name of both services. In the same letter Clinton attempts to muddy the waters by stating that Cornwallis had implied that on the arrival of Washington's troops he had been prevented from breaking out by Clinton's letter of 24 September,[14] but Cornwallis had made no such implication. It was Clinton's letters of the 2nd and the 6th, received in mid September, that had led Cornwallis to continue with his decision not to break out when Washington's troops arrived.

Cornwallis set sail for England on 15 December aboard the *Robust*, a 74-gun man of war convoying home a fleet of 120 merchantmen. The passage was not entirely without incident. On the 25th the *Robust* sprang a leak and began to make for the West Indies, her pumps constantly working. On the 28th, when 113 leagues east of Bermuda, Cornwallis had no option but to transfer to the *Greyhound* transport for his onward journey, but ill luck tempered by good fortune befell him.[15] On 14 January 1782, as the *Greyhound* raced up the English Channel, she was captured by the *Boulogne* privateer out of St-Malo in Brittany. Unable to make land there from the violence of the weather, and conscious how dangerous it would be to approach elsewhere the coast of France or to remain at sea, her captain agreed to his prize putting into an English port, having entered into the following certificate with his captives:

> We the subscribers, the master of and passengers on board the *Greyhound* transport from New York in North America, do hereby certify that, haveing been made prize on the fourteenth day of this instant January by the *Boulogne* privateer of and

---

[13] Ibid., 32-4.
[14] Ibid., 35-6.
[15] Benjamin Franklin Stevens, *The Campaign in Virginia: The Clinton-Cornwallis Controversy* (London, 1887-8), 1, xvii.

from Saint Maloes, [we] proceeded in the said ship under the direction of le Sieur Julien Duroutois, first lieutenant of the said privateer, in order to reach the ports of Morlaix or Saint Maloes, which by reason of the violence of the winds and weather it hath been impossible to effect, and as all the crew belonging to the *Greyhound* were removed on board the privateer and the people who were put on board of her from the privateer are quite insufficient to navigate her and she could not have resisted the violence of the winds and weather, which has now lasted three days and two nights, unless they had been assisted with the utmost exertions of the master and all the other persons on board the *Greyhound* who were capable to assist but who are thereby now becoming so exhausted and fatigued that they as well as the officers and men belonging to the said privateer are not able to continue them much longer, and as there is not quite one butt of water on board the said ship and it would be attended with the most iminent danger to the lives of all the persons who are board the said ship if, with the wind now blowing and which has the appearance of continuing and increasing, to approach to the coast of France, we therefore, in order to the preservation of our lives and the lives of all the persons who are on board of her, have earnestly requested the said Julien Duroutois to put into a near port in England to procure necessary assistance, and the said Julien Duroutois, being convinced of the necessity of so doing and the crew belonging to the privateer unanimously consenting and concurring with him, hath agreed thereto. We in consideration thereof do hereby undertake and promise that it shall in no wise be of prejudice to the owners or marinners of the said privateer concern'd in the capture but that the said ship shall be actually and faithfully reserved for their benefit and deliver'd to the said Julien Duroutois to proceed to Saint Maloes or Morlaix unless it shall hereafter be agreed upon that the same shall be sold and disposed of for their benefit in England, and we and each of us do hereby declare that we hold ourselves bound and promise upon our parole of honour that we will hereafter consider ourselves to be in the same situation as prisoners as we should have been if we had arrived in France on board the said ship.

Witness our hands near the Ram Head on the coast of England the seventeenth day of January Anno Domini 1782

CORNWALLIS

ALEX^R MERCER *Captain, Engineers*

CHEWTON *Aide de camp*

J SIMPSON *Secretary to the King's Commissioner*

A ROSS *Aide de camp*

HENRY STORK *Major*

H HALDANE *Aide de camp*

JOSEPH CLARKE *Master*

THO^S TONKEN *Captain, Navy*

[Endorsed:]

I do hereby certify and acknowledge that, in consideration of the necessities and distress set forth in the within certificate and from a conviction of the great danger which would attend my attempting to gain a port on the coast of France, I have, with the concurring opinion of my crew and in confidence of the stipulations contracted in the said certificate, voluntarily agreed to the request to go into an English port for the purpose therein mentioned.

JULIEN DUROUTOIS
Captain

FRANÇOIS FONTAINE[16]
First mate

Cornwallis arrived in London on or about 22 January. As he would have realised, Yorktown had effectively ended the Revolutionary War. On 4 March the House of Commons resolved that "it would consider as enemies to His Majesty and the country all those who should advise or by any means attempt the further prosecution of offensive war on the continent of North America for the purpose of reducing the revolted colonies to obedience by force." Commissioners were appointed

---

[16] CP: 6, 188-9. For biographical notes on all the persons named in the certificate except Stork, Clarke and Fontaine, See CP, *passim*.

by the warring parties and on 30 November 1782 they signed provisional articles. It was not, however, till 3 September 1783 that the Treaty of Paris was formally signed recognising the independence of the United States.

∞ 6 ∞

The South Carolina backcountry in mid 1780 — its occupation by the British, the character of its inhabitants, and its flora, fauna and terrain

When we come to the South Carolina backcountry, to which *The Cornwallis Papers* preponderantly relate, I myself was struck by the fact that, on extensively reading the literature on the southern campaigns, nowhere did I find a comprehensive sketch of this vast region or of the life and character of its inhabitants at the time that the British occupation began. Scattered items of information were to be found, but nowhere were they collated into an overall picture. Yet in my opinion such a picture was essential if one was to place, for example, *The Cornwallis Papers* in context and fully understand how backcountry society and the character of its inhabitants impacted on the revolutionary irregulars' barbarous conduct of the war. It is a purpose of *The Cornwallis Papers* and this essay to fill that gap.

The occupation was set in train on 18 May 1780 as Cornwallis began to march from Manigault's Plantation with some 2500 men for Camden.

By now appointed to command in the southern provinces, he describes the circumstances of his appointment in a letter of 12 November 1780: "When I came to town after the surrender, Sir Henry mention'd my going with him to the northward. I said that I was ready to serve wherever he thought fit to employ me, and had no objection to remain in Carolina if he thought my services cou'd be usefull in that province. He said something civil about the climate. On my assuring him that it was no objection, he then wished me to take this command. However painfull and distressing my situation has been, and however dark the prospect then was, it cannot be supposed that as a military man I shou'd not rather chuse to command to the southward than be third at New York ... I did not interfere in any degree with Sir Henry's arrangement [*the appointment of Brig. Gen. James Paterson as Commandant of Charlestown*], nor did I say more or express myself stronger on the subject of my own staying than I have described ..."

Crossing the Santee at Lenud's Ferry with part of his corps, Cornwallis marched up the eastern side of the river while Col. Francis Lord Rawdon with the rest proceeded by way of Monck's Corner and Nelson's Ferry. Camden was reached on 1 June.

At first named Pine Tree Hill, the village lay to the east of the Wateree about thirty-five miles from its confluence with the Congaree. Settled about 1750 and laid out in plots and streets around a square, it was now inhabited mostly by Scotch-Irish Presbyterians, whose meeting house and that of the Quakers were features of the place. Besides Joseph Kershaw's country store, it was home to saw- and grist-mills, one or more taverns, breweries, distilleries, a pottery, and various other artisan shops. Nine years earlier a courthouse had been built. All in all, trade was brisk and by now the village had become a principal entrepôt for the back settlements.

Politically, occupation of Camden was of course inevitable, but militarily its location left much to be desired. As Rawdon remarked many years later, "Camden had always been reprobated by me as a station, not merely from the extraordinary disadvantages which attended it as an individual position, but from its being on the wrong side of the river and covering nothing, while it was constantly liable to have its communication with the interior district cut off."

Headquarters at Camden was established in Joseph Kershaw's mansion. He was a leading incendiary.[1]

As Cornwallis approached Camden, Lt. Col. Nisbet Balfour began his march for Ninety Six, a village which lay to the south of the Saluda River some sixty miles west of its confluence with the Broad. In the backcountry it was second in importance to Camden. Leaving Charlestown on 26 May, Balfour commanded a mixed corps of some 600 men comprising three companies of the 7th Regiment (the Royal Fusiliers), a detachment of light infantry, the Prince of Wales's American Regiment, and Major Patrick Ferguson's American Volunteers. His advance along what was once an Indian trading path is minutely set out in Allaire's Diary as read with Balfour's correspondence in *The Cornwallis Papers*. Ninety Six was reached by Balfour and Ferguson's men on 22 June.

The backcountry is an amorphous expression describing the vast swathe of territory now entered by the British. Though other interpretations are wider or more restrictive, it is used here to refer to the then Districts of Camden and Ninety Six. In the east the outer boundary began at the confluence of the Congaree and Wateree, extended northwards to the North Carolina line, continued westwards along that line to the Cherokee nation, and followed the Georgia line to a point just below Augusta. From there it proceeded in the south to a point on the Saluda midway between the village of Ninety Six and the Broad River before following the Saluda and Congaree eastwards.

Today the backcountry presents a very different aspect from that encountered by the first white settlers in the middle of the eighteenth century. It was then a region interspersed with extensive plains widely covered by cane; with open forests of elm, hickory, oak, pine, poplar and walnut, between which lay

---

[1] For a biographical note on Joseph Kershaw and his brother Ely, see Ian Saberton ed:, *The Cornwallis Papers: The Campaigns of 1780 and 1781 in the Southern Theatre of the American Revolutionary War*, 6 vols (Uckfield: The Naval & Military Press Ltd, 2010), 1: 144.

a rich carpet of peavine; and with numerous ponds, rivers and streams, along which stretched vast canebrakes. It was partly flat, partly undulating, and partly hilly terrain, which rose to the Great Smoky Mountains in the distance. It abounded in many species of game ranging from bison, deer and elk to turkeys and other wildfowl. Common were the beaver, muskrat, opossum, raccoon, and squirrel. Among beasts of prey, the bear, polecat, puma, wildcat, and wolf were numerous, while the rattlesnake was widely to be found. Edible fish such as the shad were prolific.

By 1780 the backcountry had become dotted with small farms and settlements, but much of the landscape remained as it was thirty years earlier. The bison and elk had been hunted to extinction there, but the other wild animals were still to be found, though in diminished numbers.

The backcountry had yet to evolve into a uniform society. Of the national groups the Scotch-Irish were the most numerous. Disliked by others, they were aggressive, courageous, emotional, fiercely intolerant, hard-drinking, and in many cases inclined to indolence. Of the other groups the Germans from the Palatinate, who had settled mostly in the Dutch Fork, predominated. Better farmers, they were pacific, law-abiding, temperate, and devoted to the ideal of a well-ordered society. The rest were composed of other immigrants from the Old World or their descendants, a number of whom — less than ten percent of the back inhabitants — were slaves. Clannishness, through which many clung tena-ciously to their cultural heritage, was the order of the day, while mutual dislike or suspicion more often than not triumphed over brotherhood and charity. Not a melting pot, the backcountry was more akin to the Tower of Babel.

By 1776 the proportion of South Carolina's population living above the fall line had soared to some 83,000, fifty percent of its entire population and seventy-nine percent of its white inhabit-ants. By the opening of the seventies the small farm had become the means by which ninety-five percent of the backcountry settlers made a living. Nevertheless, clearing land and developing a farm involved too much backbreaking toil for some, who contented themselves with a small corn patch and hunting. Overall, the backcountry had begun to produce an amazing amount of grain and meat, and towards the end of the colonial era as many as 3,000 waggons per year were being sent down from there to Charlestown.

Living in log cabins or primitive shelters on the edge of western civilisation, very many backcountry settlers no longer conformed to accepted standards of behaviour. Criminality, immorality, and irreligion were rife, accentuated by the severe shortage of clergymen and the lack of education. Admittedly, odd meeting houses were to be found, for example at Bush River, Camden, the Dutch Fork, Fair Forest, Fishing Creek, Turkey Creek, and the Waxhaws; itinerant preachers came and went; but in general the vast majority of the population caught neither sight nor sound of a minister. "In the back parts of Carolina," recalled Major George Hanger many years later, "you may search after an angel with as much chance of finding one as a parson; there is no such thing — I mean when I was there. What they are now, I know not. It is not impossible, but they may have become more religious, moral, and virtuous since the great affection they have imbibed for the French. In my time you might travel sixty or seventy miles and not see a church or even a schism shop[2]. I have often called at a dog-house in the woods, inhabited by eight or ten persons, merely from curiosity. I have asked the master of the house: 'Pray, my friend, of what religion are you?' 'Of what religion, sir?' 'Yes, my friend, of what religion are you — or to what sect do you belong?' 'Oh! now I understand you; why, for the matter of that, *religion does not trouble us much in these parts.*'" As to honesty, Cornwallis would soon observe, "I will not be godfather to any man's honesty in this province."

---

[2] meeting house.

The ignorance and illiteracy of most backcountry settlers went hand in hand with a lack of intellectual curiosity. According to the Reverend Charles Woodmason, "Few or no books are to be found in all this vast country," besides a few religious works. "Nor do they delight in historical books or in having them read to them ..., for these people despise knowledge, and instead of honouring a learned person or any one of wit or knowledge, be it in the arts, sciences or languages, they despise and ill treat them."

Quite a few of the settlers would once have been the orphaned or neglected children who swarmed over the backcountry on the eve of the Revolution. Described as then living "expos'd in a state of nature", they had been "oblig'd almost to associate with villains and vagabonds for subsistence."

Of the few meeting houses most were attended by Scotch-Irish Presbyterians, who surpassed all other sects in bigotry and fierce denominationalism, going to lengths which are almost unbelievable. Men of God, their ministers brought politics into the pulpit, exhorted rebellion, and in some cases — for example the Reverend John Simpson of Fishing Creek — took up arms themselves.

Scattered among the backcountry population was a body of hardy, illiterate and lawless backwoodsmen whom the British came to fear more than most. They tended to have no settled habitation and lived partly by hunting and partly by preying on their neighbours. "This distinguished race of men," declared George Hanger, "are more savage than the Indians and possess every one of their vices but not one of their virtues. I have known one of these fellows travel two hundred miles through the woods, never keeping any road or path, guided by the sun by day and the stars by night, to kill a particular person belonging to the opposite party. He would shoot him before his own door and ride away to boast of what he had done on his return ... I speak ... of that heathen race known by the name of *crackers*."

Despite the vaunted levelling spirit of the backcountry, a gentry of sorts had arisen composed of the wealthy who had acquired extensive land holdings, merchants, surveyors, lawyers, and men of status in other fields. Few though they were, their influence was profound, but sadly for the British almost all were of the revolutionary persuasion.

An endemic vice in all ranks was the excessive consumption of alcoholic liquor. Rough cider and peach or apple brandy were common beverages, rum was consumed in large quantities, but rye whiskey, favoured in particular by the Scotch-Irish, was the grand elixir. Except the temperate Germans, who preferred their beer, almost everyone drank to excess: the morning bevvy, the dinner dram, the evening nightcap, and the more or less frequent tipple in between times. Taverns, still houses, and drinking cabins did a roaring trade, whereas stores commonly held among their stock a pretty liberal quantity of something to keep the spirits up.

A recurring problem was incursions by native Americans, which led to savagery on both sides. The settlers' experiences with such intermittent warfare would soon be reflected in the equally merciless way in which revolutionary irregulars behaved toward their loyalist neighbours.

Amid the hardships of backcountry life a high old time was had with recreational pursuits. From the simple pleasures of hunting and fishing they extended to horse racing and shooting matches, but more often than not they centred around the tavern, where drunkenness, gaming, cheating, quarrelling, and brawling were commonplace, particularly on days when court or other public business was transacted. Completing the picture were communal harvest days, dances, and occasions such as musters and vendues, all of which gave ample rein to the wild frolicking common on the frontier.

Of the factors that had led about half of the backcountry settlers to remain loyal to the Crown, a combination of three predominated. Partly it was a sense of belonging to a wider British community besides being Americans; partly it was a feeling of gratitude to the Crown for the grant of land; and partly it was antagonism to the low country élite, whose gross neglect of the backcountry only a few years earlier had turned many settlers against them and the revolutionary cause which they came to espouse. Admittedly, a framework of local government had recently been established, representation in the legislature was lately secured, but memories of past grievances were long.

Now divided politically, as well as in other ways, the backcountry was a place where emotions often ran free, unrestrained by concepts of civilised behaviour. A powder keg waiting to explode, it would be ignited by the coming of the British.

Bibliography

Anthony Allaire, "Diary," Appendix to Lyman C Draper, *King's Mountain and its Heroes* (Cincinnati, 1881).

Carl Bridenbaugh, *Myths & Realities: Societies of the Colonial South* (reprint, New York: Atheneum, 1976).

John Abney Chapman and John Belton O'Neall, *The Annals of Newberry* (Newberry SC, 1892).

William Henry Foote, *Sketches of North Carolina, Historical and Biographical, illustrative of the Principles of a Portion of Her Early Settlers* (New York, 1846).

Robert Gray, "Colonel Robert Gray's Observations on the War in Carolina", *The South Carolina Historical and Genealogical Magazine*, XI (July, 1910), 139-159.

George Hanger, *The Life, Adventures, and Opinions of Col. George Hanger* (London, 1801).

George Howe, *History of the Presbyterian Church in South Carolina* (Columbia SC, 1870).

J B O Landrum, *Colonial and Revolutionary History of Upper South Carolina* (Greenville SC, 1897).

Henry Lee, *Memoirs of the War in the Southern Department of the United States* (Revised edition, New York, 1869).

John H Logan, *A History of the Upper Country of South Carolina* (Columbia SC, 1859).

Ian Saberton ed., *The Cornwallis Papers: The Campaigns of 1780 and 1781 in the Southern Theatre of the American Revolutionary War*, 6 vols (Uckfield: The Naval & Military Press Ltd, 2010).

Charles Stedman, *History of the Origin, Progress, and Termination of the American War* (London, 1792).

Henry Alexander White, *Southern Presbyterian Leaders* (New York, 1911).

Charles Woodmason, *The Carolina Backcountry on the Eve of the Revolution*, edited by Richard J Hooker (Chapel Hill: University of North Carolina Press, 1953).

∞ 7 ∞

The prowess of American riflemen:
a mystery now solved

In his *Colonel George Hanger to all Sportsmen, and particularly to Farmers and Gamekeepers* (London, 1814) Hanger retails a diverting anecdote about the prowess of American riflemen, but, ever since, the date and precise location of the incident to which it relates have remained a mystery:

> Colonel Tarleton and myself were standing a few yards out of a wood, observing the situation of a part of the enemy which we intended to attack. There was a rivulet in the enemy's front, and a mill on it, to which we stood directly with our horses' heads fronting, observing their motions. It was an absolute plain field between us and the mill, not so much as a single bush on it. Our orderly-bugle stood behind us, about three yards, but with his horse's side to our horses' tails. A rifleman passed over the mill-dam, evidently observing two officers, and laid himself down on his belly, for in such positions they always lie to take a good shot at a long distance. He took a deliberate and cool shot at my friend, at me, and the bugle-horn man.[1] Now observe how well this fellow shot. It was in the month of August and not a breath of wind was stirring. Colonel Tarleton's horse and mine, I am certain, were not anything like two feet apart, for we were in close consultation how we should attack with our troops, which laid 300 yards in the wood and could not be perceived by the enemy. A rifle ball passed between him and me. Looking directly to the mill, I evidently observed the flash of the powder. I directly said to my friend, "I think we had better move or we shall have two

---

[1] Hanger adds in a footnote, "I have passed several times over this ground and ever observed it with the greatest attention, and I can positively assert that the distance he fired from at us was full four hundred yards."

or three of these gentlemen shortly amusing themselves at our expence." The words were hardly out of my mouth when the bugle-horn man behind us, and directly central, jumped off his horse and said, "Sir, my horse is shot." The horse staggered, fell down, and died.

The anecdote provides certain clues as to the date and precise location of the incident: the month was August; Hanger and Lt. Col. Banastre Tarleton were serving together in the British Legion; they were on ground that Hanger traversed on several occasions; and they were preparing to attack. So when and where did this conjunction of events occur?

Hanger was appointed major in the British Legion in June 1780 and his active service ended in October of that year when he fell ill with yellow fever at Charlotte. Therefore we can fix the month of August as being August 1780 in South Carolina. My biography of Hanger[2] details the ground that he covered during that month and from it may be gleaned the only instance in which he and Tarleton, while preparing to attack, served together during August on ground that Hanger traversed on several occasions — ground that included a mill. Taken together, these circumstances pinpoint 18 August and White's Mill on Fishing Creek as the date and place at which the incident occurred, that is to say, during their pursuit of Brig. Gen. Thomas Sumter. It was a location that Hanger traversed, not only then, but on his return from the action, and also on the Legion's advance towards North Carolina during the autumn campaign. In no other circumstances did this entire conjunction of events occur. By contrast Hanger's march from Charlestown to Camden earlier in August had covered ground over which he passed only once.

Hanger is emphatic that never in his life did he see better rifles than those made in America or men who shot better. "They

---

[2] See Ian Saberton, *George Hanger: The Life and Times of an Eccentric Nobleman* (Tolworth: Gloucester House Publishing, 2018).

are made," he says, "in Lancaster and two or three neighbouring towns in that vicinity in Pennsylvania. The barrels weigh about six pounds two or three ounces, carry a ball no larger than thirty-six to the pound, and are three feet three inches long. I have often asked what was the most they thought they could do with their rifle. They have replied that they thought they were generally sure of splitting a man's head at 200 yards, for so they termed their hitting the head. I have also asked several whether they could hit a man at 400 yards. They have replied certainly, or shoot very near him,"[3] as indeed is evinced by Hanger's anecdote.

Hanger contrasts the American rifle with the British Brown Bess: "I do maintain that no man was ever killed at 200 yards by a common soldier's musket *by the person who aimed at him*. A soldier's musket, if not exceeding badly bored and very crooked as many are, will strike the figure of a man at 80 yards; it may even at 100 yards; but a soldier must be very unfortunate indeed who shall be wounded by a common musket at 150 yards, *provided his antagonist aims at him*; and as to firing at a man at 200 yards with a common musket, you may just as well fire at the moon and have the same hopes of hitting your object."[4]

Nor does Hanger have much respect for the marksmanship of the British soldier, offering "some remarks respecting the training of a raw countryman, or a mechanic from Birmingham, perfectly awkward and generally very ignorant. He is consigned to the superintendence of the drill serjeant. He is first taught to walk, next to march, and hold himself tolerably erect. Then a firelock is placed in his hands, which he handles at first as awkwardly as a bear would a plumb cake. When he is taught the manual exercise and fit to do regimental duty, they then take him to fire powder. Whilst the drill serjeant is teaching him to fire either by files or by platoons, the serjeant says to him, laying his cane along the barrels of the firelocks, 'Lower the muzzles of

---

[3] George Hanger, *Colonel George Hanger to all Sportsmen.*
[4] Idem, *A Letter to the Right Hon. Lord Castlereagh* (London, 1808).

your pieces, my lads, otherwise when you come into action, you will fire over the enemy.' After this the recruit is taken to fire ball at a target. How is he taught? Thus he is spoken to: 'Take steady aim, my lad, at the bull's eye of the target; hold your piece fast to the shoulder that it may not hurt you in the recoil; when you get your sight, pull smartly.' This is the general way in which I believe they are taught, and in the name of truth and common sense permit me to ask you how a drill serjeant who is no marksman himself can teach an ignorant countryman or a low order of a mechanic to be a good marksman. In my humble opinion, excellent in their way as they are to discipline the soldier and form him for parade and actual service in the line, the serjeant is just as capable of teaching him how to solve one of Sir Isaac Newton's problems as to teach him to be a marksman."[5]

---

[5] Idem, *Reflections on the Menaced Invasion* (London, 1804).

∞ 8 ∞

Re-evaluating the war in the south — the importance of The Cornwallis Papers

It is extraordinary that 230 years did elapse before someone — namely myself — edited and published the material in the Cornwallis Papers relating to the southern campaigns.[1]

A very small part of the material was already in the public domain. The few dispatches between Cornwallis, commanding in the south, and Clinton, the commander-in-chief, were, for example, published in part in the *London Gazette* and elsewhere during or shortly after the war. In the nineteenth century Charles Ross published brief extracts amounting to 121 pages, and other examples have appeared elsewhere, for instance in monographs or local histories such as those by Cashin and Robertson, Pancake, and Rogers.[2] Other recent works in which brief extracts appear include, for example, biographies or partial ones such as those by Bass, Rankin, the Wickwires, and Willcox.[3] Yet, taken together,

---

[1] See Ian Saberton ed., *The Cornwallis Papers: The Campaigns of 1780 and 1781 in the Southern Theatre of the American Revolutionary War*, 6 vols (Uckfield: The Naval & Military Press Ltd, 2010) ("CP").

[2] Charles Ross ed., *Correspondence of Charles, First Marquis Cornwallis* (London, 1859), vol. I; Edward J Cashin Jr and Heard Robertson, *Augusta and the American Revolution: Events in the Georgia Back Country 1773-1783* (Augusta: Richmond County Historical Society, 1975), 41-8, 50 and 51; John S Pancake, *This Destructive War: The British Campaign in the Carolinas, 1780-1782* (reprint of 1985 edition, Tuscaloosa: University of Alabama Press, 2003), 81-3, 89, 92-4, 190, and 191; George C Rogers Jr, *The History of Georgetown County, South Carolina* (Columbia: University of South Carolina Press, 1970), 123-33, 136-38, and 142.

[3] Robert D Bass, *The Green Dragoon: The Lives of Banastre Tarleton and Mary Robinson* (reprint of 1958 edition, Columbia: Sandlapper Press Inc, 1973), 75, 76, 105-17, 121-25, 139, 140, 142-49, 151, 160, 167, 168, 175, 176, and 182; Hugh F

the extracts published before my own work comprised nothing more than a tiny fraction of the Cornwallis Papers relating to the southern campaigns. Nor, since their lodgement in the UK National Archives, was reliance placed on them in a variety of seminal works, whether, for example, they be, on the one hand, general accounts such as those by Fortescue, McCrady, Ward, Alden, and Mackesy or, on the other, biographies or monographs such as those by Robinson, Thayer, Treacy and Nelson.[4] The picture began to change on publication of *The CP*, as I shall describe later.

The CP has two purposes: first, to provide a comprehensive and fully edited transcript of the papers; and second, in view of the numberless inaccuracies published about the war, to provide a commentary, whether in the introductory chapters or various footnotes, aimed at presenting the papers in an accurate, balanced and dispassionate way.

As far as the comprehensiveness of the transcript is concerned, it is described to some degree in the Editorial method

---

Rankin, *Francis Marion: The Swamp* Fox (New York: Thomas Y Crowell Company, 1973), 49, 53-5, 65, 67, 73, 74, 78-80, 88, 90, 91, 110-12, 114-16, 121-25, 128, 130, 134, 140, 145, 190, 203, and 204; Franklin and Mary Wickwire, *Cornwallis: The American Adventure* (Boston: Houghton Mifflin Co, 1970), 132, 134, 138, 144, 147, 153, 154, 170, 171, 173-75, 178, and chs 8-12 and 14-16 *passim*; William B Willcox, *Portrait of a General: Sir Henry Clinton in the War of Independence* (New York: Alfred A Knopf, 1964), 338, 355n, 378, and 382-84.
[4] Sir John Fortescue, *A History of the British Army* (London: Macmillan & Co, 1902), vol. III; Edward McCrady, *The History of South Carolina in the Revolution* (New York: The Macmillan Co, 1901-2); Christopher Ward, *The War of the Revolution* (New York: The Macmillan Co, 1952); John R Alden, *The South in the Revolution 1763-1789* (Baton Rouge: Louisiana State University Press, 1957); Piers Mackesy, *The War for America 1775-1783* (reprint of 1964 edition, Lincoln: University of Nebraska Press, 1993); Blackwell P Robinson, *William R Davie* (Chapel Hill: University of North Carolina Press, 1957); Theodore Thayer, *Nathanael Greene: Strategist of the American Revolution* (New York: Twayne Publishers, 1960); M F Treacy, *Prelude to Yorktown: The Southern Campaign of Nathanael Greene, 1780-1781* (Chapel Hill: University of North Carolina Press, 1963); Paul David Nelson, *General Horatio Gates: A Biography* (Baton Rouge: Louisiana State University Press, 1976).

at the beginning of volume I.[5] The omission of duplicates, tripli-cates, and quadruplicates of papers appearing in *The CP* requires no further explanation, whereas the omission of odd, extreme-ly isolated papers is explained in greater detail in a footnote below.[6] Otherwise the papers relating to the southern campaigns are published in their entirety.

As important as the transcript is, of no less importance are the re-evaluations of certain crucial aspects of the war contained in the introductory chapters and various footnotes. Necessarily compressed, or else they would unbalance the work, they "very briefly provide pointers," as the preface explains. "They also address certain important considerations that have long gone by default, together with others that are equally pertinent to placing the Papers in context."[7]

Turning now to *The CP*'s place in the historiography of the southern campaigns, I shall address, first, the literature predat-

---

[5] CP, 1: xiii-xvi.

[6] Such isolated papers are stated to have been omitted on the ground that they do not relate to the southern campaigns or are too inconsequential. If we take volume I as an example, we find that, out of the mass of papers that may have appeared there, only fourteen have in fact been omitted on those grounds. Of them, seven do not relate to the war in the south, some being written before 1780, others consisting of intercepted private letters of no relevance, and one a printed resolution of Congress relating to the New Hampshire Grants (later to become Vermont). The rest are also of little consequence to the conduct of the southern campaigns or to a reinterpretation of them: an intercepted letter requesting payment for two and a half bushels of salt; an intercepted list of Captain Archibald Murphey's company of Richmond District, Orange County NC, revolutionary militia; another intercepted list of a few NC recruits to the Continental line; a private letter to Cornwallis about the appointment of a physician; the draft of a warrant (never effected) to raise a Backcountry Provincial regiment; the draft of a letter, dated May 1780, from Cornwallis to Amherst offering his services elsewhere in the world, but overtaken by his appointment to command in the south; and lastly a short list of supplies appropriated by the army from one particular plantation. It is on the same grounds that extremely isolated papers listed in later volumes are omitted there.

[7] CP, 1: ix.

ing the publication of my work, being literature apparent to me at the time that I was preparing my draft; second, the literature postdating its publication; and finally, and most importantly, the ways in which *The CP* has contributed, and is likely to continue to do so, to writing about the southern campaigns.

As to military literature predating the publication of *The CP*, a most interesting overview of that by American writers, and almost unique in its day, was provided by Higginbotham in 1964, but sadly for my purposes its scope was too wide, extending to the war as a whole. Later it was amplified by him and supplemented, among others, by Carp, Coakley and Conn, Coffman, Gephart, Greene, Harrow, Karsten, Nelson, and Syrett.[8] What follows is a synthesis of their views, as partly modified by my own so as to centre more closely on literature about military operations in the south.

---

[8] Don Higginbotham, "American Historians and the Military History of the American Revolution," *The American Historical Review*, 70, No. 1 (October, 1964), 18-34; Don Higginbotham, "The Early American Way of War: Reconnaissance and Appraisal," *The William and Mary Quarterly*, 3rd Ser., 44, No. 2 (April, 1987), 230-73; E Wayne Carp, "Early American Military History: A Review of Recent Work," *The Virginia Magazine of History and Biography*, 94, No. 3 (July, 1986), 259-84; Robert W Coakley and Stetson Conn, "A Select Bibliography of Historical Literature on the Military History of the American Revolution" in their *The War of the American Revolution* (Washington DC, US Government Printing Office, 1975), 141-244; Edward M Coffman, "The New American Military History," *Military Affairs*, 48, No. 1 (January, 1984), 1-5; Ronald M Gephart, *Periodical Literature on the American Revolution: Historical Research and Changing Interpretations, 1895-1970* (Washington DC: Library of Congress, 1971); Jack P Greene, *Interpreting Early America: Historiographical Essays* (Charlottesville and London, 1996); Stefan M Harrow et al., *The American Revolution: A Selected Reading List* (Washington DC: Library of Congress, 1968); Peter Karsten, "The 'New' American Military History: A Map of the Territory, Explored and Unexplored," *American Quarterly*, 36, No. 3 (1984), 389-418; Paul David Nelson, "British Conduct of the American Revolutionary War: A Review of Interpretations," *The Journal of American History*, 65, No. 3 (December, 1978), 623-53; David Syrett, "The British Armed Forces in the American Revolutionary War: Publications, 1875-1998," *The Journal of Military History*, 63, No. 1 (January, 1999), 147-64.

There have been three distinct periods into which American historiography of the war in the south, and indeed of the war as a whole, may be divided: the first, extending roughly to the end of the nineteenth century, was marked by rampant American nationalism, leading the reading public to seek its heroes in the war and historians to portray it uncritically in black and white terms; the second, covering the four decades till the close of the Second World War, was a phase in which both the public at large and academic historians lost much of their interest in revolutionary warfare; and the third, beginning about 1945, has seen the re-entry of the military theme into the mainstream of revolutionary studies.

Although, beginning in the nineteenth century, much primary material began to be published, some in book form, but preponderantly in American historical journals, the fact is that American histories, biographies, monographs and articles of that era were so materially unbalanced that none is addressed in this essay, being superseded to a marked degree by those published since 1945. As regards the period from the turn of the century till then, the publication of primary material continued but otherwise writing about the military history of the war in the south was sparse, though Gregorie, an academic historian, published a critically acclaimed biography of Sumter, and Williams, a gifted non-professional, produced two informative works on the overmountain settlers and their involvement in the Battle of King's Mountain.[9]

American historians were led by the Second World War to begin a vast outpouring of material on the military history of the Revolutionary War, a phenomenon that shows no signs of abating. Until then the liberal academic's prejudice against war, and by extension those who study it, had prevailed for almost

---

[9] Anne King Gregorie, *Thomas Sumter* (Columbia SC: R L Bryan Co, 1931); Samuel Cole Williams, *Dawn of Tennessee Valley and Tennessee History* (Johnson City, Tenn: The Watauga Press, 1937) and *Tennessee during the Revolutionary War* (reprint of 1944 edition, Knoxville: University of Tennessee Press, 1974).

half a century, but now it was recognised that the investigation of warfare could not be ignored.[10] No longer, as distinct from the nineteenth century, were works about the Revolutionary War to be characterised by "drum and bugle" history — the depiction of battles and actions, the relation of heroic conduct, and generally the glorification of the martial spirit, but were centred, though by no means solely, on campaigns, strategy, tactics, logistics, and weapons. And with the advent of guerrilla wars in Algeria, Angola, Cuba, Indochina, Kenya, Malaya and Vietnam there came recognition in the 1970s of the important contribution to the war effort made by revolutionary partisans, whether collectively, as in the militia, or as individuals. At the same time a "new military history" evolved. As Karsten states, it exhibited "a full-fledged concern with the *rest* of military history — that is, a fascination with the recruitment, training, and socialization of personnel, combat motivation, the effect of service and war on the individual soldier, the veteran, the internal dynamics of military institutions, inter- and intra-service tensions, civil-military relations, and the relationship between military systems and the greater society."[11]

All in all, it would be invidious in this essay to single out specific examples of this vast output when so much is relevant to military operations in the south.

When compared with works by American writers on the southern campaigns or by revolutionary participants in them, those emanating from British, loyalist or Hessian sources prior to *The CP's* publication are few indeed. We have, for example, works by Tarleton, MacKenzie, Hanger, Simcoe and Stedman in the eighteenth century, by Lamb, Gray, Allaire and Raymond in the nineteenth, and by Fortescue, Chesney, Uhlendorf, Robson,

---

[10] For a brief discussion of academic attitudes toward military history, see E Wayne Carp, "The Problem of National Defense in the Early Republic," in Jack P Greene ed., *The American Revolution: its Character and Limits* (New York: New York University Press, 1987), 14-50.
[11] Karsten, "The 'New' American Military History," 389.

Wright, Mackesy, Clinton, Ewald and Davies in the twentieth, but overall the material emanating from British, loyalist or Hessian sources is sparse, perhaps reflecting a disinclination on their part to write about a war that the British had lost.[12]

The CP was published in mid 2010 and continues in print. Not publicised beforehand, or widely afterwards, it took some time for it to become broadly disseminated among historians but is now so. By the close of 2012 works of a general nature had begun to make use of it, as had monographs, biographies,

---

[12] Banastre Tarleton, *A History of the Campaigns of 1780 and 1781 in the Southern Provinces of North America* (London, 1787); Roderick MacKenzie, *Strictures on Lt Col Tarleton's History of the Campaigns of 1780 and 1781 in the Southern Provinces of North America* (London, 1787); The Hon George Hanger, *An Address to the Army in reply to Strictures of Roderick M'Kenzie (late Lieutenant in the 71st Regiment) on Tarleton's History of the Campaigns of 1780 and 1781* (London, 1789); John Graves Simcoe, *A Journal of the Operations of the Queen's Rangers from the end of the year 1777 to the conclusion of the late American War* (Exeter, 1787); Charles Stedman, *History of the Origin, Progress, and Termination of the American War* (London, 1792); Roger Lamb, *An Original and Authentic Journal of Occurrences During the Late American War from its Commencement to the Year 1783* (Dublin, 1809) and *Memoir of His Own Life* (Dublin, 1811); Robert Gray, "Colonel Robert Gray's Observations on the War in Carolina," *North Carolina University Magazine*, 8, No. 4 (November, 1858), 145-60, republished in *The South Carolina Historical and Genealogical Magazine*, 11 (July, 1910), 139-59; Anthony Allaire, "Diary," Appendix to Lyman C Draper, *King's Mountain and its Heroes* (Cincinnati, 1881); W O Raymond, "Roll of Officers of the British American or Loyalist Corps," *Collections of the New Brunswick Historical Society*, 2 (1899); Fortescue, *History*; E A Jones ed., "Journal of Alexander Chesney, A South Carolina Loyalist in the Revolution and After," *Ohio State University Bulletin*, 26, No. 4 (1921); Bernhard A Uhlendorf trans. and ed., *The Siege of Charleston..: Diaries and Letters of Hessian Officers* (Ann Arbor: University of Michigan Press, 1938); Eric Robson, *The American Revolution in its Political and Military Aspects 1763-1783* (reprint of 1955 edition, New York: W W Norton & Co Inc, 1966); Esmond Wright, *Fabric of Freedom 1763-1800* (London; Macmillan & Co Ltd, 1965); Mackesy, *The War for America*; William B Willcox ed., *The American Rebellion: Sir Henry Clinton's Narrative of His Campaigns 1775-1782* (New Haven and London: Yale University Press, 1954); Joseph P Tustin trans. and ed., *Diary of the American War: A Hessian Journal* (New Haven and London: Yale University Press, 1979); K G Davies ed., *Documents of the American Revolution 1770-1783*, vols. XVIII and XX (Dublin: Irish Academic Press Ltd, 1978-9).

and articles in historical journals — a trend that has continued.[13] No serious work about the war in the south can fail to take into account *The CP* if it deals with British strategy, tactics, the British response from their perspective to the nature of the conflict and the problems faced by them, the royal militia, the administration of South Carolina outside Charlestown, the policies pursued and the reasons for them, and various other matters on which the contents of *The CP* throw light.[14] Nevertheless the transcripts, emanating, as they do, almost entirely from British or British American officers and officials, inevitably view, through the prism of their own polarised perspectives, policies, events, and the actors in them. While we can, for example, accept at face

---

[13] For example Daniel T Canfield, "The Futility of Force and the Preservation of Power: British Strategic Failure in America, 1780-83," *Parameters* (US Army War College Quarterly), 42, No. 3 (Autumn, 2012); Carl P Borick, *Relieve us of this Burthen: American Prisoners of War in the Revolutionary South, 1780-1782* (Columbia: University of South Carolina Press, 2012); William T Graves, *Backcountry Revolutionary: James Williams 1740-1780* (Lugoff SC: Southern Campaigns of the American Revolution Press, 2012); Llewellyn M Toulmin, "Backcountry Warrior: Brig. Gen. Andrew Williamson," *Journal of Backcountry Studies*, 7, Nos 1 and 2 (Spring and Fall, 2012); Paul E Kopperman, "The Medical Dimension in Cornwallis's Army, 1780-1781," *The North Carolina Historical Review*, 89, No. 4 (October 2012); C L Bragg, *Crescent Moon over Carolina: William Moultrie and American Liberty* (Columbia: University of South Carolina Press, 2013); Andrew O'Shaughnessy, *The Men Who Lost America: British Command during the Revolutionary War and the Preservation of the Empire* (London: Oneworld Publications, 2013); John C Parker Jr, *Parker's Guide to the Revolutionary War in South Carolina*, 2nd ed. (West Conshohocken PA: Infinity Publishing, 2013); Daniel Murphy, *William Washington, American Light Dragoon: A Continental Cavalry Leader in the War of Independence* (Yardley PA: Westholme Publishing, 2014); Daniel T Canfield, *Understanding British Strategic Failure in America: 1780-1783* (Charleston SC: Createspace, 2014); Wayne Lynch, "The Making of a Loyalist," *Journal of the American Revolution* (January 2014); idem., "Elijah Clarke and the Georgia Refugees fight British Domination", ibid. (September 2014); Jim Piecuch, "Richard Pearis and the Mobilization of South Carolina's Backcountry Loyalists", ibid. (October 2014); Wayne Lynch, "Moses Kirkland and the Southern Strategy," *Southern Campaigns of the American Revolution* (April 2015); William Thomas Sherman, *Calendar and Record of the Revolutionary War in the South: 1780-1781*, 10th ed. (Seattle WA: Gun Jones Publishing, 2015); John R Maas, *The Road to Yorktown* (Charleston SC: The History Press, 2015).

[14] See, for example, Kopperman, "The Medical Dimension."

value Cornwallis's contention at Charlotte that the county of Mecklenburg was the most rebellious that he had met with in America, we may look askance at Lt. Col. George Turnbull's unbalanced description of inveterate Scotch-Irish revolutionaries and the way in which he recommended that they be treated if captured:[15] "Those Mecklenburgh, Roan, and my friends the Irish above are perhaps the greatest skum of the Creation. English lenity is thrown away when there is not virtue to meet it half way. If some of them could be catched who have submitted and run off and join'd the rebels, an example on the spot of immediate death and confiscation of property might perhaps make them submit." So, when we use the transcripts to illuminate the past, we need, inevitably, to think about bias in the sources, recognising that they are not transparent or innocent documents but are written in particular circumstances and for particular audiences. "Reading against the grain" is therefore at times essential, though generally, when we interpret the war, we need, as ever, to view it not just through the prism of the present but also through that of the past.[16]

Where then is the overall place of *The CP* in the historiography of the southern campaigns? As previously stated, it comprises both transcripts and a commentary on various aspects of the war in the south. As to the former, it is a continuation not only of works by Ross, Stevens, and Davies but, more importantly, of the recently published *Greene Papers*, being those of the Continental general opposed to Cornwallis in late 1780 and early 1781.[17] As such, the transcripts provide not only the views and decisions of Cornwallis and Clinton but also those of the Commandant of

---

[15] For a biographical note on Turnbull, see CP, 1: 138-9.
[16] CP: I, 364, and II, 106; John H Arnold, *History* (London: Oxford University Press, 2000), *passim*.
[17] Ross ed., *Cornwallis Correspondence*; Benjamin Franklin Stevens ed., *The Campaign in Virginia:...: the Clinton-Cornwallis Controversy*, 2 vols. (London, 1887-88); Davies ed., *Documents*; Richard K Showman, Dennis M Conrad, Roger N Parks, et al. eds, *The Papers of General Nathanael Greene*, vols VI to IX (Chapel Hill: University of North Carolina Press, 1991-97).

Charlestown and of subordinate officers in command of posts or regiments. Besides highlighting the problems faced by the British and the measures taken to resolve them, they include much other information, for example on logistics and the care of the sick or wounded. All in all, they provide a far more rounded and informed picture than one emanating from the British high command alone.

As regards my commentary in *The CP*, it is preponderantly concerned with matters other than those that the "new military history" addresses and on which *The CP* throws only marginal light. *Ipso facto*, the commentary adopts a more traditional approach, forming conclusions on the nature and events of the war and the actors in it.

If I were to summarise the overriding importance of *The CP*, I would point to the opportunity that it affords historians to address in a much more knowledgeable way the big questions and, in doing so, to consider the answers to them given in, or inferable from, my commentary. My first essay is a case in point.

Lightning Source UK Ltd.
Milton Keynes UK
UKHW05n2333280518

323292UK00001B/1/P